GROW FRUIT & VEGETABLES IN POTS

GROW FRUIT & VEGETABLES IN POTS

PLANTING ADVICE & RECIPES FROM GREAT DIXTER

Aaron Bertelsen

Photographs by
Andrew Montgomery

INTRODUCTION

I am lucky enough to have plenty of space for growing fruit and vegetables. Yet it is one of the smallest corners of the garden – the kitchen courtyard – that perhaps brings me the most pleasure.

This small area, just a few metres square, with its mellow brick walls and floor, sits directly outside my kitchen door. In Christopher Lloyd's day, it was simply a threshold between house and garden – a place to knock the mud off your boots, prop up a spade or fork, or set down a heavy trug full of freshly dug produce.

But over the past few years, it has become rather more than that. When you spend as much time at the kitchen sink as I do, it is very important to have something nice to look at. I started by introducing a few pots of delicate species tulips – beautiful, but what to do with the space when they died back in the early summer? Herbs seemed the obvious answer. A few leftover seedlings of parsley, dill and coriander (cilantro) were tucked in where the tulips had been, and I very quickly came to appreciate the benefits of having these things close to hand when cooking, to throw into a salad or add a burst of fresh green flavour to a dish.

Next, I decided to raise the stakes a bit. I had been wanting to grow something tall that would look good next to the kitchen door and, of course, be useful in the kitchen too. My friend Perry, who also works here at Great Dixter, gave me an old salmon net he had found in a junk shop. I put it in a large plastic pot full of good rich soil, popped a few leftover 'Australian Butter' bean seeds (see page 77) around the base, and a few weeks later had the most wonderful obelisk of scrambling greenery, followed a little while later by the delicious beans themselves.

Then I decided to put some terracotta pots planted up with leftover lettuce, kale and leek seedlings from the garden around the base to conceal the plastic – and so my own container garden began to take shape.

Today the courtyard is a thriving kitchen garden in its own right, with fruit, vegetables, salads, herbs and flowers yielding crops pretty much all year round. It is a visual treat, and the most wonderful cook's pantry. There really is nothing better than wandering out while the potatoes are boiling to pick a few sprigs of mint to accompany them, or serving a bowl of freshly picked salad leaves (greens) you have grown yourself. A handful of cherry tomatoes straight from the vine, chopped and stirred into a bowl of pasta, needs nothing more than a splash of good olive oil and a twist of fresh black pepper to make a supper fit for a king. And if you have never tasted peas popped straight into your mouth within seconds of picking, I would go so far as to say you haven't lived.

Much has been said and written of late about the importance of understanding where our food comes from, of shifting the focus of our meals to include more vegetables, and reducing food waste. I believe that growing your own – or at least some of your own – is one of the most effective ways of changing your attitude to what, and how, you cook and eat. Eating seasonally, and making the best use of your ingredients, seems to come more naturally when they are growing right outside your door, and that is very much the focus of the recipes in this book. I am a great believer, too, in the psychological benefits of gardening. There is something immensely calming about caring for and nurturing plants, no matter how small the scale.

With this book, I hope to show that lack of space is no barrier to being able to enjoy the pleasure of growing – and eating – your own. Far from being limiting, container gardening offers endless possibilities. A sheltered courtyard creates a microclimate, where it is possible to grow crops such as apricots and peaches that might struggle in a more open site. Sun-worshippers, such as tomatoes, chillies and aubergines (eggplants), will thrive on a bright balcony, while shadier spots are ideal for salad crops, potatoes, leafy greens such as Swiss chard, and fruits, such as blueberries, rhubarb and even currants. Meanwhile, woody Mediterranean herbs, such as rosemary and thyme, can cope with the most inhospitable conditions.

One of the great advantages of container growing is that it is easy to extend the growing season. Many plants will benefit from the additional warmth found close to the house or apartment, and it is the work of a few seconds to throw a piece of fleece (see page 231) or hessian (burlap) over more vulnerable pots.

Another bonus of container gardening is that there is no back-breaking digging, and you are free to create different compost (potting soil) mixes to suit the needs of individual crops – light soil for carrots and parsnips, acidic for blueberries and so on. A container garden also provides opportunities to grow unusual varieties or hard-to-obtain ingredients, such as that obscure herb you need for your favourite curry but can never seem to find in the shops.

While this book draws heavily on my own experiences of growing container crops at Great Dixter, I am also endlessly inspired by others. My good friend Cornelia's garden is the example I always turn to when people try to tell me they don't have space to grow their own. Her magical garden, grown entirely in containers, is proof that with a little effort and imagination, even the tiniest space can become a place of wonder. Then there is my friend Laura, whose restrained and harmonious courtyard has shown me that less is almost invariably more. It is difficult to think of any nicer way to spend an evening than eating

supper there, surrounded by simple terracotta pots filled with mint, pelargoniums and citrus trees, which are particularly fragrant when in blossom.

Different as they are, what both of these spaces have also shown me is that a container garden can be a thing of beauty. Of course, beauty comes in many different guises, and I love to see how people manage to grow fresh fruit and vegetables in tricky places. I think of Jo, whom I met on a trip to the Barbican in the heart of London, making her own compost and growing fresh salads and greens year round in a concrete trough and some window boxes in an apparently inhospitable part of the inner city. Or my friends Lior and Ayala in their small apartment in Jerusalem, packing their tiny balcony with plastic troughs full of fresh herbs and salad leaves. Or Nigel and Anthony, whose urban riverside balcony is home to a healthy and productive apple tree growing happily in a wheelie bin (tall trashcan).

Ultimately, though, wherever you live, and whatever the scale and type of space you are working with, the process has to be enjoyable. In this book my aim is to show that with very little planning and effort, growing and cooking your own fruit and vegetables can be an immensely pleasurable and rewarding experience. I hope it will inspire you to create your own container garden.

THE CONTAINER KITCHEN GARDEN

The Container Kitchen Garden

CHOOSING WHAT TO GROW

Making the decision what to grow might sound simple, but it is absolutely fundamental to the success of your garden. Choose crops that are not suited to your site, or that don't reflect what you use in your cooking, and the chances are you will quickly lose interest – and there is nothing sadder than a neglected container garden. The goal is to create a space that brings you pleasure, not to mention crops, all year round.

WHICH CROPS CAN BE GROWN IN POTS?

The short answer to this question is, anything you like. From delicate leafy herbs to root vegetables and sturdy fruit trees, there should be no reason why – given a little thought, forward planning and, of course, some tender loving care – you can't create a varied, productive container garden, whatever the space and the conditions you are working in.

If I could grow only one type of thing in my container garden, it would be salad leaves (greens). This also happens to be what I would recommend new gardeners to start with. Salad leaves are easy to grow, make good use of space and generally taste much better than what you can buy in the shops. A couple of 30-cm/ 12-inch pots of cut-and-come again leaves will give you flavoursome fresh salads for weeks, if not months. I'm convinced home-grown salad leaves are more nutritious, and they also look beautiful. Choose carefully and you will have a pot full of textures and colours to bring you pleasure throughout the year.

Other stars of the kitchen container garden include stalwarts like chard and kale, which will keep you in fresh greens all year round; structural plants, such as globe artichokes, that will anchor your display; and true showstoppers, such as peas and the gloriously varied sea kale. You will find that many of them offer tremendous value too. Some, such as chard, will just keep on growing, while others offer several crops for the price of one: think of peas, with their shoots, flowers and juvenile pods, or the delectable tops (greens) of broad (fava) beans.

Root vegetables may not seem like the most obvious candidates for a container garden, but they can do very well in a confined space, and, of course, you can control the growing conditions in a pot far more easily than in a garden. They are also surprisingly generous crops to grow: a pot of beetroot (beets) will give you handfuls of delicious leaves (greens) as well as the roots themselves. Root vegetables are well worth growing for aesthetic reasons too: the bright green, frothy foliage of a carrot is a great foil for the dramatic, deep red of beetroot leaves, while parsnips are so good-looking that we actually grow them as flowers in the ornamental garden at Great Dixter.

Think about growing fruit, and the first thing that comes to mind will probably be an orchard, or at the very least a generous kitchen garden. Think again. These days there are so many dwarf forms of fruit trees especially bred to thrive in pots – and produce full-size fruit – that there really is no reason not to grow your own. Indeed, having limited space can actually work to your advantage – walls, provided they get plenty of sun, will reflect heat and speed up ripening, particularly of more exotic crops, such as figs, apricots and peaches. But even if a tree feels too ambitious, you can still share the joy. A blueberry bush in a pot will yield handfuls of sun-warmed berries, while delicate, violet-flavoured Alpine strawberries don't even need a pot of their own – they will happily grow in the spaces around other crops, or even in the cracks between paving slabs.

Herbs are generally very well suited to growing in pots. They take up relatively little space – although do avoid using containers that are too small (see page 23) – and give so much in return. A few fresh herbs will transform your cooking, and I do believe that home-grown versions taste better and more intense than their shop-bought counterparts.

To my mind, edible flowers are the icing on the cake of the container garden; even just a few flowers will make it sing with their colour and scent. Another great thing about them is that, once they are established, they will self-sow, creating a wonderful visual effect. And they will attract pollinators too, helping to make the rest of your garden more productive.

PRACTICAL CONSIDERATIONS

Perhaps the single most important consideration in choosing what you are going to grow is time. It is very easy to get carried away when flicking through seed catalogues or browsing at a nursery or garden centre, but remember – crops need sowing, pricking out, watering, feeding, pruning, protection from pests ... the list goes on.

It is not my intention to put you off, but if you're new to container gardening, my advice is to start small – perhaps with a pot of salad leaves and another with a mixture of the herbs you use most often. Early successes will fuel your appetite to do more with the space you have.

The next step is to look at your space. Size is the most obvious consideration. If you are really limited – to a windowsill, a tiny balcony or a small area just outside a door, for example – there is no point thinking about creating a container fruit orchard. But what you can do is have a generous pot each of, say, your three favourite herbs. Even a container garden on this scale will enhance your space, and add a new dimension to your cooking.

Then look at the conditions. How sunny is your space? How exposed is it? Where does the prevailing wind come from? A reasonably sunny, moderately sheltered spot will, of course, open up more possibilities for growing a wider range of crops, but inhospitable conditions need not be a deal-breaker (see page 21).

While I am a fervent advocate for growing your own, there is little point if you're not going to make use of the crops. It is well worth taking some time before you start sowing and planting to think about what you love to eat, and what you really need and want for your kitchen. Think in terms of quality rather than quantity. You might get only four apricots all summer, but what apricots they will be, and how rewarding to eat them knowing that you grew them yourself.

For me, salad leaves are probably the number one priority (see page 17). Herbs are another essential – I use them so much in my cooking, and it is hard to come by generous, good-quality bunches of herbs in the shops. Also, commercially grown herbs often come from nutrient-poor soil, which means they lack the rich flavour of those you grow yourself. My must-have herbs include coriander (cilantro), because I love the seeds as well as the leaves, and basil. Even if you get only a month from your crop, it is a month of pure pleasure.

I would also include sorrel in my essential line-up, as it is almost impossible to buy. The flavour is so strong and distinctive that you need only a little to make a soup or bring life to a salad. Many people find its astringency off-putting, but this illustrates the real benefit of growing your own – you are completely free to cultivate what pleases you.

While favourites always top the list, think variety too. You don't want to go overboard, particularly in the early days of container gardening, but growing a range of crops will ensure that you always have something interesting to pick and to eat, and – crucially – something to look at. You can even extend the growing season through succession sowing – sowing small amounts of seed at intervals rather than all at the same time – to ensure continuity of both crops and visual interest.

It's also worth considering whether to grow things that add lots of flavour to dishes, but are expensive to buy. Aubergines (eggplants), borlotti (cranberry) beans, heritage tomatoes, pea shoots and forced rhubarb are excellent examples. In fact, grow your own peas and you get not only the tender shoots, but also wonderful fresh peas. With these, the sugars in them start to turn to starch as soon as they are picked, so the sooner you have them podded (shelled) and in the pan, the better. Just a handful tossed through pasta with some fresh mint and parsley will make a perfect supper. Like peas, broad beans quickly lose their freshness once picked, so are another candidate for growing yourself.

You could also consider growing things that are fragile and difficult to transport, such as berries. Once you have had a handful, still warm from the sun, sprinkled over your cereal in the morning, you will never go back to buying them from the supermarket.

GETTING THE BASIC LAYOUT RIGHT

A container garden offers enormous flexibility: if a pot is in the wrong place, you can simply pick it up and move it. Nevertheless, it is well worth taking the time to consider how best to use your space in order to maximize productivity and minimize backache.

THE LOGISTICS OF THE SPACE
Start by looking around your plot and thinking about the space you have available. Apart from growing things, what else do you need or want from it? If a balcony is also a fire escape, it will need to be kept clear. If you have slightly more space and enjoy eating outside, which is the best spot for your table and chairs? If you have children, where does their play equipment go? Do you need to move bins (trashcans) in and out,

or leave clear access to a door or gate? Will you also use the space to hang out laundry? Once you have answers to these considerations, you can start to look at what space you have left for plants and decide what should go where.

One of the great things about gardening in an enclosed space is the scope for gardening vertically as well as horizontally. Berries will thrive against a wall, which will reflect light and heat from the sun to create a microclimate, and fan-trained specimens make efficient use of limited space. Arches and pergolas, too, can be used to support climbing plants, such as beans and even pumpkins (note that bigger fruit might need little hammocks to support them), freeing up more space for crops at ground level and also increasing exposure to the sun.

of shade. Big-leaved vegetables, such as lettuce, chard and spinach, will happily grow in partial shade – indeed, full sun will quickly dry them out and encourage them to run to seed. Beans, beetroot (beet), leeks and kale will also tolerate some shade, as will currant bushes.

Wind is a major consideration, particularly in elevated or exposed sites, such as balconies or roof terraces. Screening can help to protect plants from the worst, but do bear in mind that it could also cut out light. Hardy Mediterranean herbs, such as rosemary and thyme, will thrive in sunny, windy spots, and the tough conditions will even intensify their flavour. On the other hand, delicate leafy crops, such as Swiss chard, spinach and salad leaves (greens), will need more shelter. Looking on the bright side, a good breeze is the enemy of many common plant diseases, including mildew and blight (see page 231).

Don't be afraid of a little trial and error. It might take you a few seasons to find the right position for each crop, but that is the beauty of growing in pots – you can just keep moving them around until you get it right.

As I've seen in my friends' container gardens, the space limitations can lead to great creativity and bring a sense of fun to a small area. Planters and shelves can be attached to the wall, and pots can be arranged on ladders or steps. In Israel, my friends grow herbs in plastic bottles hanging from the windowsill, and you can easily double the growing space in a window box by hanging pots from it (do make sure they're securely attached, though). In a slightly larger space, bring your most attractive pots close to the house. It is so important to be able to look out of the window and take pleasure in what you see.

THE NEEDS OF THE PLANTS

How much sun, shade and wind does your space receive? Not all plants have the same needs, so by understanding your environment, you can work out how to make the most of its strengths, mitigate any problems and give your plants the best possible chance.

Many crops, including most fruits and tomatoes, will need sun for much of the day if they are to thrive, while others are more tolerant

CREATING THE BEST EFFECT

When arranging my pots, my aim is always to avoid things looking flat and static. Think contrast: bright orange flowers next to glaucous leaves; purple and bright green foliage side by side; or broad shiny leaves next to something fine and feathery. Try to vary the height too. Just as in the garden, it is not always the case that the tallest plants should be at the back, although you must be careful not to let a giant specimen block out all the light. Something like dill, which offers height but also transparency, is ideal. Plant supports such as obelisks or wigwams (see page 48) make great punctuation points too.

The Container Kitchen Garden

CHOOSING CONTAINERS

Rather like deciding what pictures to hang on your walls, choosing containers for your plants is a very personal thing. At Great Dixter, the majority of our pots are terracotta. They sit well against the brick floor and walls of the courtyard, and they age gracefully. Aesthetics aside, though, more or less anything can be used to grow crops in as long as it has sides to hold the soil in place, and holes in the bottom to allow for drainage.

The one thing that is critical about your chosen pots is size. Small pots can look very pretty clustered together and will enable you to create more variety in small spaces, such as steps and tabletops, as well as being easier to bring inside during the winter, but bear in mind that they will dry out very quickly. I am lucky – I work in a garden and there is always someone who can water the pots when I'm not around, but that is not typical. You do not want to be spending all your spare time watering, nor do you want to be such a slave to your pots that you can't go away on holiday. One large pot containing three or four different varieties of plant grown together will be much easier to maintain than multiple pots, and give much greater visual impact too. Remember, you don't need to fill the entire pot with compost (potting soil) – you can put a layer of something light and bulky, such as perlite, at the bottom, then put your soil on top of that (see page 28).

The shape of pot you choose depends on what you plan to grow in it. For salad leaves (greens) or herbs, which have shallow roots, choose a broad, shallow pan rather than a tall, narrow pot so you're not wasting the space in the lower part of it. So-called 'long Tom' pots are best used for plants with deeper roots and/or trailing foliage, such as carrots, parsnips, nasturtiums, trailing rosemary, trailing thyme and trailing cherry tomatoes.

If you want to grow a fruit tree, choose the biggest pot you can accommodate. This will allow your tree plenty of room to expand, and you can grow other crops around the edge of the pot. Provided you are diligent about feeding and top-dressing (see page 44), your tree will need repotting (see page 56) only once every four or five years, rather than every spring.

When you are just starting out, my advice is to keep things simple. A single trough with, say, sorrel, some cut-and-come-again salad leaves, and a few of your favourite herbs will be easy to look after and give you so much pleasure. Add a few edible flowers to the mix and you will have something that's really beautiful to look at too.

TERRACOTTA POTS

Rather like supermodels, terracotta pots look good anywhere, but the best can command eye-watering prices. While you can get cheap alternatives, the more expensive pots will repay the investment – they are properly frost-proof and will last for years, gaining a wonderful patina in the process. Terracotta is excellent for drainage and won't overheat, as water evaporates through the porous clay, creating a cooling effect. On the other hand, this means they need frequent watering. Weight can be an issue too, especially if you are using terracotta for plants that are likely to need moving around. In this case, you can reduce the weight by filling part of the space at the bottom of the pot with perlite, or putting plants in plastic pots inside the terracotta, using a brick to raise them to the required height as needed.

STONE POTS

If you've ever travelled in Italy, you will probably have seen plants being grown in beautiful stone pots. I always come home full of plans to try to recreate the effect. Then I remember that while stone may be beautiful, long-lived and excellent for moisture retention, it is also extremely heavy and expensive – much more so than even good-quality terracotta. If you do use stone, you can do something to mitigate the weight, if not the cost, by packing the bottom with perlite, or planting into a plastic container, then dropping this inside the stone container. Also, just as with terracotta, you can cheat by having a few beautiful pots at the front of your display and putting everything else in plastic.

CONCRETE POTS

An excellent alternative to stone, concrete is much cheaper and will take on a mellow patina with age. While classic designs are available, simpler and more streamlined pots are also an option. Concrete works especially well in urban and modern settings, where stone might look ostentatious or out of place. Another way in which concrete resembles stone is its weight. You can reduce the weight by filling part of the space at the bottom of the pot with perlite.

PLASTIC POTS

Plastic pots are light, cheap and retain water well. However, plastic has a detrimental effect on both land and sea when carelessly discarded, so we all need to be more careful and considerate. I try to do my bit by reusing my plastic pots over and over again, and I recommend you do the same. If storing them is a problem, look online for local recycling schemes, which will help to keep the number of newly made pots to a minimum.

The other big drawback to using plastic is its appearance. Of course you could learn to live with it, but I prefer to hide my plastic pots – and

yes, I do have them – behind the terracotta, or even inside it. Another solution is to paint your pots, and there are lots of online tips for how to tackle this, though be careful what's in your paint so you don't get nasty chemicals going into the compost. The painted surface won't last forever, but it will look good for at least a few years, and as it ages the flaking paint can look quite attractive too – sort of shabby chic.

Plastic is great for crops like tomatoes and beans, where a terracotta pot of the appropriate size would be prohibitively expensive and too heavy to move. With plastic, you can keep a pot display looking its best by moving shabby but still productive plants to the back. Equally, if a plant is looking particularly good, you can easily shift it to the front and give it a chance to shine.

METAL POTS

While metal containers are relatively lightweight, they are very durable. The big challenge is to prevent them from overheating, especially in a warm climate or a particularly sunny spot. Planting into plastic, or lining metal containers with a layer of bubble wrap, will help to insulate roots and prevent them from being damaged by extremes of temperature.

Most metal plant pots nowadays are made of galvanized zinc, which has a timeless appearance that looks great, especially in an urban setting. However, old tin cans and tin bathtubs can be turned into attractive planters that will enhance any small outdoor space.

FABRIC GROWING BAGS

I am a total convert to fabric growing bags. They are light – making them ideal for anyone growing on a balcony or terrace, easy to move and will last several years. They also come in an amazing array of sizes, including ones big enough to grow squashes or potatoes. A large one is almost like a portable raised bed, and can be used to grow a number of different crops simultaneously.

Fabric growing bags offer good drainage and there is even evidence to show that they encourage the development of healthier root systems. Added to that, when not in use, they are easy to fold up and store. Oh, and did I mention that they are cheap too?

WOODEN CONTAINERS

While wooden containers, such as old apple crates, are fun to use and look picturesque, do bear in mind that anything made from untreated wood will soon rot if kept outside. For this reason, think salad leaves rather than perennial crops. Line wooden containers with hessian (burlap) to stop the soil spilling out and, ideally, raise them off the ground so that they are not sitting in water (do watch out for slugs if you decide to do this, though). Avoid anything made from tanalized (pressure-treated) timber as the chemicals used in the process will leach into the soil and contaminate the crops.

CERAMIC POTS

It has to be said that ceramic pots are not the most practical option. They are heavy, often expensive, tend not to be frost hardy and often lack drainage holes, although these can be drilled. (Be careful to use the right drill bit or better still take your pots to someone who knows what they are doing.) However, they can be very beautiful and make a wonderful centrepiece for your garden. A great way of using a ceramic pot is to put the plant in a plastic or fabric pot inside it. This allows the plant to be lifted out for watering, and thus prevents it from becoming waterlogged.

RECYCLED AND REPURPOSED CONTAINERS

Old watering cans, buckets, food containers, sinks and wheelbarrows – you can use more or less anything to grow fruit and vegetables. Apart from being a great way of introducing some colour and character to the container garden, they're cheap and look good in almost any setting – imagine some beautiful olive oil cans planted up with herbs on the windowsill. That said, do proceed with caution because recycled containers can contain traces of their former use, including substances that could be harmful to plants and people. Clean them thoroughly before planting.

TOOLS & EQUIPMENT

Very little equipment is needed for container gardening. A decent hand fork, a good sharp trowel – I like the Sneeboer brand, made in the Netherlands and sold at (among other places) Great Dixter – and a watering can with a fine rose are pretty much all you will need. Add some decent secateurs (pruning shears) – my favourites come from Japan and are as simple as can be (just two pieces of forged metal and a spring), so there is nothing to go wrong, and they hardly ever seem to need sharpening. A ball of decent twine will be useful too.

You may also want to add a pair of gloves to your toolkit. I've got into the habit of wearing them all the time. If you are cooking as much as I do then it is a real boon to be able to keep your hands clean, not to mention beautifully soft. I like the thin, stretchy type of gloves, so I can still feel what I'm doing.

Even with a kit this small, though, you will need to decide where to keep it when you're not working, as not everyone wants to turn their kitchen into a toolshed. One solution is an outside bench with storage space underneath, which will double up as a vantage point from which to sit and admire your handiwork. Other options to consider include using a plastic pocket hanger (like those for storing shoes) that can be hung from a hook indoors or out, or a small plastic box that can double as a surface on which to stand pots.

I store my kit in an old wine box – one of those nice wooden ones with a sliding lid, which provides a perfect – and very appropriate – spot to rest my glass at the end of the day.

Finally, all good gardeners need a notebook. It's well worth keeping track of what seeds you buy, when you sow and plant out, and what performs well or not. When it comes to the start of the next growing season, it will be a really useful reference point and help you to avoid repeating your mistakes.

SOIL & COMPOST

There is a bewildering range of composts (potting soils) available on the market, from ericaceous (acidic) mixes for acid-loving plants to those designed for citrus trees, but essentially the choice comes down to one of two options. You can choose either a soil-based mix, or one based on peat or – increasingly these days – a peat substitute, such as composted bark, coir or wood fibre. The ubiquitous multipurpose compost falls into this second category.

We are lucky at Great Dixter to have the space and means to make our own soil-based compost mixes, which derive from the recipes originally developed at the John Innes Centre in Norfolk. I use these for everything from sowing seed to potting perennial plants. It is great stuff, rich in nutrients and very easy to water, unlike multipurpose composts, which, once they have dried out, can be impossible to re-wet.

No matter how limited your space, it is perfectly possible to make small amounts of your own compost, but loam- or soil-based composts are widely available commercially.

SOIL-BASED COMPOST

Typically, you will find three types of soil-based compost available in nurseries and garden centres:

• No. 1, for sowing seed
• No. 2, for potting on small plants
• No. 3, for long-term and permanent plantings

The main difference between the three types is the level of nutrients they provide, with No. 1 containing no added nutrients at all and No. 3 being the richest.

Sold alongside these you will also find multipurpose composts that contain added nutrients, but soil-based mixes are always a better bet. Their structure means they retain nutrients for longer, and they are also much more similar to the actual soil in which plants would grow naturally. The structure also provides for excellent drainage: plants have the opportunity to draw up the water they need without them then sitting with their feet in a puddle of water.

The one great disadvantage of a soil-based mix is weight, which may well be an issue if you are growing on a roof terrace or balcony.

MULTIPURPOSE COMPOST

Multipurpose compost can be used for everything from sowing seeds to planting trees, but it is a much inferior option to soil-based compost. While it weighs much less, multipurpose compost makes bigger demands in terms of both feeding and watering. If you do use it, check the bag carefully to see how long the fertilizer it contains will last, and be vigilant about feeding right from the start. Top-dress with organic matter or worm compost (see page 44) and use a good feed, such as liquid seaweed, otherwise you will get a marvellous first crop, but subsequent plantings will be disappointing.

THE BEST CHOICE

Whatever your choice, when planting seeds I recommend using a compost mix specially prepared for sowing seed. Seed compost (seed starting mix) usually comes in small bags, and its fine texture and good moisture retention are designed to encourage germination and healthy growth. I always use it when I am sowing seed into small pots for subsequent pricking out (see page 35). For direct sowing – that is, sowing seed where it will grow to maturity – it's fine to use your regular compost.

It's also pretty much essential to use a soil-based compost for perennial plants, such as trees and shrubs, because these long-lived plants need the nutrient- and water-holding properties of soil if they are to thrive. And if you are planning to grow acid-loving plants such as blueberries, you must use an ericaceous compost, or the plants will be unable to access the nutrients in the compost and eventually starve to death.

Some plants, particularly woody herbs such as rosemary and thyme, but also dill, scented-leaf pelargoniums, lemons and sea kale, will benefit from having some sharp sand or horticultural grit mixed into the compost to make it more free-draining. In winter, they are far more likely to die from wet than cold, so aim to add about one part sand to nine parts compost when you are filling the pot before planting.

MAKING YOUR OWN COMPOST

It's not difficult to make your own compost, and there are three easy ways of doing this using either kitchen waste or fallen leaves and pine needles.

• **The Bokashi system** – This system, which originated in Japan, uses a special bran inoculated with beneficial bacteria to effectively pickle kitchen waste, giving off a liquid that can be diluted with water and used as a feed. Of course, it also creates organic matter, which can be put into the bottom of newly planted pots. The system works very well in a small space, as I discovered when I recently met a wonderful gardener called Jo, who uses it to make compost in a small space outside her apartment in central London. To speed up the process, she puts her kitchen waste through a blender before combining it in a bucket with the special bran. After a couple of months she has beautiful crumbly compost, which she uses to top-dress her window boxes, thus continuously enriching the soil.

• **Wormery** – Worms are another great option for making compost. On a recent trip to Melbourne, Australia, I met a fantastic vegetable gardener, Joost Bakker, who is currently setting up a rooftop urban farm and runs seven waste-free restaurants. He reckons the best thing you can do for your soil is to have a wormery. It's a great way of disposing of your own food waste – or, indeed, the pickled solids from your Bokashi bucket. The worms will digest the waste to create a beautiful, rich compost that can be used for feeding and top-dressing, and yet more fine liquid feed. In winter, move the wormery under cover, if possible – a shed is ideal – or cover it with hessian (burlap) or bubble wrap to insulate against the worst of the cold.

• **Leaf mould** – Rotted down leaves and pine needles are another excellent resource, and very simple to make at home, provided you have a secluded corner. Just put a pile of leaves into a black plastic sack, tie the top and punch a few holes in it to let air circulate. Set it aside and leave to rot for two years – a commitment in terms of time and space, but worth it. You can use the resulting leaf mould as a mulch for top-dressing pots, or add it to compost when you are planting.

SEEDS & PLUG PLANTS

There is absolutely no shame in buying plug plants instead of growing things from seed. Having said that, some things are so easy to grow from seed – salads, carrots, peas, coriander (cilantro), dill, parsley – that it seems a great shame not to give it a try. Growing from seed is very cost-effective and will give you the widest choice of varieties, but it is time-consuming and doesn't always go to plan.

SEEDS

One of my great pleasures during the winter is to sit down with a selection of seed catalogues and start making lists for the following year. I am a sucker for a beguiling description, particularly when it relates to how well a vegetable cooks or its excellent taste. This is not to say that I don't care how things look. Indeed, I will often choose a variety, say a yellow courgette (zucchini) or a purple climbing bean, specifically with contrast and visual interest in mind. But flavour always comes first.

After that it is worth considering the other information given in the catalogue or on the seed packet. Growing conditions, for example, are very important. If a vegetable needs full sun and you have a shady courtyard, it's not going to thrive. Check sizes too. There is no point trying to grow giant pumpkins in a pot, or some older varieties of climbing plants, such as peas, which get very tall indeed. While many of these older seed varieties – often called heritage or heirloom – are great performers, I am with Christopher Lloyd, who always used to say there was a reason why many of them had fallen out of favour. Older is not always better. If I think the best variety is a modern hybrid (look for 'F1' on the packet), that is what I will choose.

The more I learn about how seeds are produced, the more inclined I am to opt for organic seeds. The rules restricting the use of chemicals on plants grown for food crops do not apply to plants grown for seed, and that gives me cause for concern. To me it makes sense if you are growing something that is ultimately going to be on your plate to start with clean seeds, ideally from small, local producers. Alternatively, you can save your own seed (see page 53), which is easy and economical, but you do need to make sure that the seed is coming from healthy plants.

PLUG PLANTS

Much as I love growing vegetables from seed, even I have to admit that it can be hard work. To get from seed to healthy young plant will require a fair bit of your energy, attention and space. The alternative is to buy plug plants – young plants in individual cells – which you simply pop out and plant straight into your pots. Buy them from nurseries or garden centres in the spring to ensure the widest choice of vigorous young plants.

Obviously, this is not the most cost-effective way of growing vegetables – and you won't get such a wide choice of varieties as if you were growing from seed – but it is very efficient. Most plug plants come in trays of six, which is an ideal number for the container garden. Try to plant them up as quickly as possible because the compost (potting soil) they are in will be fast running out of nutrients by the time they are big enough to be sold. It is also a good idea to shake off the peat they have been growing in or they will struggle to establish themselves in a soil-based mix.

You will not need to worry about hardening off the plants if they are growing in the outdoor section of the garden centre. Just pop them out of the cells and into holes you have made in the compost in your pots, firm them in and water well. You can also intersperse plug plants with crops that are best sown direct. Mixing, say, plug lettuces with direct-sown coriander or dill will make your pot more interesting and also maximize the available space.

SOWING SEEDS

Spring is the peak seed-sowing time, but see the individual crop-by-crop growing guides (pages 58–109) for specific sowing recommendations. I sow most things into 7.5-cm/3-inch pots, and the first step is to make sure they are clean. The next step is to buy a bag of good seed compost (seed starting mix) (see page 29). Don't be tempted to compromise and use multipurpose instead – it contains nutrients your seeds don't need, and the texture is harder for the seedlings to push their way through.

Fill the pots almost to the top with compost and tamp it down by tapping the pots firmly against a hard surface, or lightly pressing it with your hand. Be careful not to compact it too much, as this will interfere with drainage, and also make it harder for the roots to develop. The aim is just to get rid of any air holes and to make sure the compost doesn't sink too much when you first water the pot, leaving the seeds exposed. One way to ensure against this is to water the compost and allow that water to percolate through before sowing. This is a useful thing to do anyway when sowing seeds such as beans, peas, sweet peas, courgettes (zucchini) and squashes, which are prone to rotting if left sitting in too much water.

Once the surface is level, sprinkle the seed over it sparingly. Remember that each seed is a potential plant, and if they are too closely packed, they will start to strangle each other and you will find it difficult to thin them out without causing damage. Finish with a thin covering of seed compost – ideally, about twice the depth of the seed itself. Try to make sure the soil is at the same level in all the pots. This will help you to water evenly.

Then – assuming you have not already watered the compost underneath – water the pots, ideally outside on the ground. Fill your watering can and start by watering the ground next to the pots, only moving the rose over the pots once you

can see that the water is flowing smoothly and gently, otherwise an initial spurt of water can dislodge the seeds. Put them somewhere that will get plenty of light – the windowsill is perfect.

Now they will need covering. This can be done by putting them in a small propagator – essentially a tray with a clear plastic covering. This will give you better control over temperature and moisture levels, the two factors that are critical to germination.

Most propagators have small vents that you can open to increase air circulation. Open the vents on particularly sunny days, to avoid overheating, and also if you start to see moss growing on the surface of the soil. You can also use the vents to reduce condensation; a little condensation dripping back onto the soil will help keep it moist, but too much will lead to the fungal disease known as damping-off (see page 231). Propagators make it easy to water pots from the bottom, avoiding the risk of washing seeds away or damaging emerging plants. When the time comes to harden off the seedlings (see page 36), all you need to do is remove the lid and take the tray outside.

If you're not using a propagator, cover each pot with clingfilm (plastic wrap), or use small, clear plastic bags to make a kind of cloche over each one, securing them with an rubber band. You probably won't need to water the pots, as condensation from the plastic cover will drip down and keep them moist, but do check regularly and give them a gentle sprinkle if they start to look dry. As soon as you see the first signs of green, whip the covers off so that air can circulate. This will help to prevent damping-off.

DIRECT SOWING

Of course, you can also sow many seeds directly into their 'forever' position. Depending on the crop, the weather and when you are sowing, some direct sowings will benefit from being covered with fleece (see page 231) to get them going. Direct sowing is more risky, as the tiny plants will be exposed to the dangers of the outside world, but it is a lot less labour-intensive. As with sowing into small pots, make sure the surface of the prepared soil is even, sow sparingly and cover seeds with a thin layer of earth before watering them in with a fine rose.

The Container Kitchen Garden

PRICKING OUT

Once you can see the first true leaves – that is, the leaves of the plant itself rather than the cotyledons or 'seed leaves' that emerge first (see page 231) – you will need to prick out (separate) the seedlings. Don't leave it too late, or they will get tangled and be difficult to separate without damage.

Start by knocking both compost (potting soil) and seedlings out on their side, into a tray. Then tease the seedlings apart, either with your fingers or using a pencil or thin stick. You can use the same tool to make holes in your plugs or pots of tamped-down compost (see page 32). Pick each seedling up by its leaves – *not* the stem or you may damage the plant – and drop it into a hole. Make sure the soil doesn't cover the foliage, but do bury the stem as far as possible, using a stick to help push the compost if you like. This will help the plants to grow sturdy and bushy, rather than leggy and weak.

I like to prick out seedlings into plug trays because the individual cells will allow you to see when roots start coming out of the bottom, the sign that your seedlings are ready to plant out. Plug trays do tend to be quite large, but you can cut them up into sections, or put multiple crops into the same tray. Just remember to label them carefully.

Of course, you can also prick out into pots – the same ones you used to sow the seed – putting three or four seedlings into each pot. Try to give them about the same amount of space as if they were going into a plug tray. Whatever you are using, the young plants will still need to be protected from the elements at this point. Keep them inside on the windowsill, unless you have some covered growing space outside. Good light is crucial, and it's important to turn the trays or pots regularly so that all the seedlings are getting equal exposure.

HARDENING OFF & PLANTING

Once you start to see roots emerging from the bottom of the plug tray or pots, there should also be plenty of strong, healthy growth on top. This is the time to ready your plants for their final position by helping them to acclimatize to the outdoors.

Leave the tray or pots outside during the day to start with, and take them in at night. Use a layer of fleece (see page 231) if the weather is particularly harsh. After a week of this, your plants should be ready to be planted out.

The ideal time to plant out is when rain is forecast, but don't delay if the plants are ready. It's very important to keep them moving because if they run out of space or nutrients where they are, they will stop growing, and you will find it very hard to get them going again. If you are concerned about the cold, you can always protect them with some fleece. Start by putting some broken crockery or chunks of broken pot in the bottom of the pot or container you want to plant into. Fill with good soil-based compost (potting soil) (see page 28), firming it down as you go to get rid of any air pockets. Use a trowel to make a space for each plant – check the seed packet for the correct spacing – and pop them in. Try to plant to the same level as the plants were in the previous pot. Firm the soil around them and water in well.

As the seedlings start to grow, keep an eye on them to make sure they are not becoming congested: as well as hampering their growth, this will lead to poor air circulation and damping-off (see page 231). Thin out to ensure that each seedling has a bit of breathing space around it. You may need to do this several times as the plants grow so that eventually each seedling is left with enough space around it to reach its mature size. Don't throw the thinnings away – try adding them to a salad for a pop of fresh flavour.

The Container Kitchen Garden

COMBINING CROPS

One of the great things about using generous-size pots is that they give you scope to grow different crops together, extending the cropping period for the container and creating some really exciting combinations of texture and colour. Mixing and matching can be great fun – for example, think speckled green and red lettuce alongside deep green parsley set against the electrifying orange of marigolds. It's really not difficult to create a space that is attractive and inviting, but there are some practical considerations too.

SPEED OF GROWTH

It's important to ensure that not all the plants are growing at the same rate, otherwise they will crowd each other out. Radishes are very useful here, because they grow so quickly. Sprinkle a few around your lettuces and they will be ready to eat in time for the growing lettuces to then expand into the space that's freed up. Similarly, you can plant other crops around the base of perennial plants – perhaps lettuces around globe artichokes, or creeping thyme around the base of a blackcurrant bush.

HEIGHT

When combining crops, consider height. It might sound obvious, but don't grow climbing beans in the same pot as a fruit tree unless you actually want it to be smothered. But if you are growing beans, why not add a few sweet peas? In this case, the height of the plants will be complementary and the flowers will add colour and scent, as well as helping to attract pollinators. Companion planting will make your garden more beautiful and more productive.

SOIL

The more plants you have in a pot, the greater the demands you are making on the soil. That is why it is so important to use a good compost (potting soil) with plenty of nutrients, such as John Innes No. 3 (see page 28), and to make sure that you are feeding your pots regularly with a good,

all-round fertilizer, such as liquid seaweed, and top-dressing with something nutrient-rich, such as worm compost (see page 44).

GOOD COMPANION PLANTS

Apart from looking good together, certain combinations of plants can even provide a healthier growing environment. Here are a few tried-and-tested combinations that look beautiful and also grow well together:

- Mediterranean herbs, such as rosemary, thyme and lemon thyme. Apart from looking good, rosemary is useful for deterring cats, and a handful of crushed lemon thyme is good for repelling mosquitoes.
- French marigolds with mixed salad leaves (greens) – the flowers help to deter whitefly (see page 233).
- Tomatoes and basil – because they are so often eaten together.
- Figs and thyme – a great flavour combination.
- Fruit trees and nasturtiums – the flowers will attract aphids (see page 233) and keep them away from your other plants.
- Purple kale with French marigolds – the flowers help to repel beetles.
- Carrots with chives – the herb helps to deter carrot fly.

'FILLER' PLANTS

The following also make perfect 'filler' crops to put around other plants, either because they tend to grow fast and be used up quickly, or because if they grow too quickly and take over – nasturtiums, I'm looking at you – you can simply rip them out, safe in the knowledge that they will grow back before you have time to miss them:

- Violas (these pretty flowers look wonderful paired with parsley).
- Radishes (perhaps the quickest-growing of all).
- Lettuces.
- Soft herbs.
- Nasturtiums.

SHRUBS & FRUIT TREES

Shrubs and fruit trees are a great way of bringing year-round interest to the container garden. There is blossom in the spring, fruit in the summer and autumn and structure throughout the winter – you could even decorate them with strings of fairy lights at Christmas if you are that way inclined. At other times of year your shrubs or trees can double up as a plant support – a few sweet peas or a couple of ipomoea (morning glory) plants will look lovely twining through the branches of an apple tree, for example. You could even try using a tree as a support for an edible climber such as French (snap) beans – just be careful not to smother the tree by planting too many. Then, too, there is the sense of achievement you will get from harvesting your own fruit. Salads are great, but fruit really does take container gardening to a new level.

VARIETY

When it comes to selecting a variety of fruit tree, the first thing to check is that it is grown on dwarfing rootstock (see page 231). All fruit trees consist of two parts – the top, which produces the blossom and fruit, and the roots, which determine the overall size. Note that the fruit will be the same size regardless of the ultimate size of the tree. Look for phrases such as 'patio' or 'dwarf form' to guide you towards a tree that won't be bursting out of the pot within a couple of years.

With both trees and shrubs, think about when they're going to fruit. However tempting the description in the catalogue, there is no point choosing a variety that ripens in the month you always go away on holiday. I also advise you not to be too wedded to the idea of having an heirloom variety. Modern breeders have worked hard to develop varieties that are adapted for growing in pots, and you will get better results with one of these. Most are self-fertile too, meaning that they will pollinate themselves and are not dependent on being close to other fruit trees.

Indecisive gardeners can hedge their bets by choosing one of the new types of apple or plum tree with multiple varieties grafted onto a single trunk. (They are called fruit salad trees – a marvellous name!) We had an apple tree like this when I was growing up in New Zealand, and it was fantastic. It's a great way to enjoy more than one variety – say, a cooking apple and a dessert apple – and to get a longer fruiting season.

FORM, NOT SIZE

If you are shopping in the real world rather than online, and therefore have the luxury of selecting your own plant, focus on form, not size. This is a lesson I learned from Christopher Lloyd, who was a great believer in starting small and giving the plant an opportunity to get established, rather than always going for immediate impact. The biggest plant won't necessarily be the best performer in the long run, but a plant with a balanced and appealing shape will bring you pleasure for many years to come.

If you are planning to grow your tree flat against a wall, either fan-trained or espaliered (see page 231), you should be looking for a strong central leader with an even number of branches either side. If it's going to be freestanding, make sure it looks good from every angle. Look for healthy bark and leaves, rejecting specimens that are damaged or callused. Just as with tools, buy the best you can afford.

BARE-ROOT OR CONTAINER-GROWN?

The first decision you will have to make when selecting a shrub or tree to grow in a pot is whether it should be bare-rooted or container-grown. Bare-root plants, as the name suggests, come as they are, with nothing around their roots but a wrapping of plastic, paper or hessian (burlap) to stop them drying out. They are grown in fields, then dug up in the autumn, and are available to buy only in winter.

Bare-root plants are tougher, cheaper and offer a greater choice of varieties, so this is the way to go if you can. But if your site is particularly cold or exposed to winter winds, it might be safer to wait until later in the season before putting out a new plant. In this case, you might have to go for a container-grown specimen, which is more expensive and fussier too, having spent its whole life being mollycoddled in a pot rather than toughing it out in a field. While container-grown trees are theoretically available all year round, you will have a better choice if you go shopping in spring or autumn. My preference would be to buy and plant in spring so that the tree or shrub has a whole season to grow and get established before the colder weather sets in.

POTTING UP

Whichever option you choose, it is important to get your plant potted up and outside as soon as possible. In the case of bare-rooted plants, you will have no choice but to do this immediately, so make sure you have the pot and soil ready (see below). With container-grown plants, there can be a temptation to leave them in their original pot for a while. Don't do it. Although they might look healthy when they arrive, the compost (potting soil) around them could well be running short on nutrients.

Plant into an appropriate-size pot (see page 23) and a good soil-based mix (see page 28). I like to add some enriching organic matter, such as leaf mould or compost, and a little horticultural grit to aid good drainage. Pack the soil down well; it doesn't need to be solid, but you do need to get rid of any pockets of air. It is also important to get the level right: the graft line – where the top part of the tree meets the rootstock – should be about 5 cm/2 inches above the level of the soil in the pot, otherwise there is a risk that the top part of the tree – the non-dwarfing part – will start to form roots itself and try to grow too big.

Once your plant is potted up, stake your tree (see page 46). Start watering and feeding immediately and note that if you do opt to wait until the weather is warmer before potting a plant up, you will need to be extra-diligent about watering until it gets established.

The Container Kitchen Garden

WATERING & MULCHING

Watering is perhaps the single most important garden activity, yet few people know how to do it really well. Plants in containers are much more vulnerable to drying out than those in the ground. Your choice of pot and the compost (potting soil) you use will make a difference of course, but there are no shortcuts to be taken here. You must water, and water well.

Bearing this in mind – along with the fact that, depending on the size of the pot, the type of soil and the crop, you may find yourself watering every day in the summer – it is worth trying to make the job as easy as possible. If space permits, install a water butt (rain barrel) or two to collect precious rainwater. If tap water is not easily accessible, consider putting in an outside tap (faucet). Buy a decent-quality hose, and make sure it's long enough to reach every corner of your growing space.

I cannot emphasize enough the importance of having a good infrastructure in place before you begin. Make it as simple and as pleasurable as you can, otherwise you will find yourself skimping on the job, and all the effort you have put in thus far to sow and nurture your plants will be wasted.

So, how often to water? The short answer is, it varies. (For crop-by-crop advice, see pages 58–109.) Some plants – lemon trees spring to mind – like to dry out completely in between waterings and will need attention only once a week or so. Others, such as tender salad leaves (greens), will need watering every day. It depends on the size of the plant and whether it is tender and green or tough and woody. Think too about a plant's natural habitat: for example, plants that thrive in hot, dry Mediterranean conditions, such as rosemary and thyme, will not respond well to too much water.

Whether you are watering daily or weekly, or somewhere in between, your aim should always be to ensure that the moisture has penetrated a good way down the pot. Ideally, the soil inside would be absolutely drenched. If you water properly, you'll need to do it less, as the roots will be longer and stronger and better able to access moisture – and nutrients – further down the pot. The simplest way to check is to stick your finger in the pot to test how far down the moisture has gone.

One very effective way to water pots that are small and light enough to lift is to submerge them so that the surface of the soil is under water, and leave them for 30 minutes or so. If you are watering seedlings from the top, remember to use a fine rose on your watering can.

You can water with ordinary tap water, but the lime it contains will build up in the soil over time and this can be detrimental, particularly to acid-loving plants. If your water supply is metered, it can be expensive too. So-called 'grey' water, the run-off from bathing and washing, can be saved in buckets and butts, and is an environmentally friendly alternative, provided you are using a biodegradable soap. As a child, I remember seeing my grandmother catching the water from the washing machine and using it on the garden. A little extreme, maybe, but then she did have plenty of time on her hands.

Mulching your pots in spring will help to seal in moisture and reduce the need for watering. You can use a good thick layer (about 5 cm/2 inches) of leaf mould or straw. Just pile the stuff on top of the compost, but do keep an eye on it as it will rot down fairly quickly, and top it up if needed. You can also use cardboard as a mulch; it doesn't need to be 5 cm/2 inches deep, a single layer of cardboard is fine, as long as it covers all the soil.

If you are going away for any length of time – say, more than a couple of days – you will have to persuade someone to water for you. Do make sure you train them properly beforehand, and give the pots a good drenching yourself before you go. Again, the bigger the pot, the more forgiving it will be. If you decide to let nature take its course, you run the risk of coming back to a dead or dying garden. The only crops that will thrive on this kind of treatment are hardy Mediterranean herbs, which will actually get better and more intensely flavoured if starved of water. I suppose that would be some consolation.

FEEDING

Most commercial compost (potting soil) mixes include a slow-release plant food, which will typically last between four and six weeks. After that, you're on your own. It's a good idea to get into the habit of feeding your containers regularly – weekly is ideal – from the start. Note that they will only need feeding while they are putting on growth, not when they are dormant.

I use liquid seaweed, an excellent feed for all crops, simply adding it to the watering can. I do it on the same day each week so that I don't forget. Despite its name, tomato food is also a great all-round fertilizer, and is available in both liquid and granule forms. The granules will need to be forked in and then watered. Both a Bokashi composting system and a wormery (see page 29) will generate fertilizing liquid, as well as compost and organic matter. This makes an excellent and very nutritious feed.

Apart from their weekly feed, plants will also benefit from being top-dressed, which means adding organic matter to the surface layer of the pots. Start by checking the soil level in the pot; if it is high, scrape some off, then sprinkle in a few handfuls of a fertilizer, such as blood, fish and bone meal (see page 231), which will help to promote strong roots, as well as healthy foliage and fruit. After that, add fresh compost – ideally, worm compost or leaf mould (see page 29) – to bring the soil in the pot back up to its original level.

WEEDING

It is just as important to weed containers as it is to weed garden beds because the intruders will compete with your plants, depriving them of their fair share of water, nutrients, light and space. It's important to keep on top of this task, and not let things get into too much of a tangle.

You can help make the task easier by always planting into a clean growing medium, by which I mean a good-quality commercial compost (potting soil) mix, ideally soil-based (see page 28). Don't go digging up soil from other people's gardens or the local park. Equally, if you are planning to use organic matter, try to make sure it's as free from weeds as possible. In a large compost heap, for example, the heat generated by the composting process will kill off a lot of seeds, so you won't get them regrowing when you eventually use the compost. It's also worth avoiding muck (manure) or compost that's been stored in a place where weed seeds can blow in from the surrounding area. If that can't be avoided, simply take your compost or muck from the lower layers of the pile, as most weeds will be on the surface. Dense planting can also keep down weeds by reducing the space available for them to grow. We use this technique throughout the garden at Great Dixter, whether we are planting in the ground or in pots.

No matter how careful you are, though, there will still be weeds. You can use a hand trowel or fork to dig them out, or just pull them up with your fingers. However, do be careful, as you may well find that the roots are entwined with those of your seedlings or plants. It can also be difficult when seedlings are very small to tell the difference between the plants you want and those you don't. The trick is to identify the ones that all look the same; the weeds should be the rogues and easy to pick out, unless you have a particularly bad case. If in doubt, wait a bit until your vegetable plants are big enough for positive identification.

SUPPORTING PLANTS

If you want to support your plants effectively, it is important to know their natural growing habit, and nearly as important is to plan ahead. There is no point waiting for plants to be flattened by the wind before you decide to put in a support. By then the damage is done. Where they will be needed, supports should be put in place at the same time as you are sowing and planting.

So how do you know if a support is going to be needed? The three main factors to consider are height, weight and fragility. Anything that grows very tall will definitely need support. This includes crops such as climbing beans and peas, which also score highly on the fragility scale. Tomatoes, too, will need some help, particularly by the time they are bearing fruit, when all the weight will be at the top of the plant, leaving the stem vulnerable to snapping. The same is true of aubergines (eggplants), if you are lucky enough to get them to ripen.

Broad (fava) beans, although relatively short, bear a lot of weight on a fragile stem. Kale, too, may need a bit of support, particularly if your site is exposed to the wind, as will taller varieties of edible flowers, such as marigolds. Trees of all varieties will need staking, particularly in the early years, before their trunks have bulked up. And, of course, espaliered or fan-trained trees (see page 231) will need support throughout their lives to help maintain their shape.

The next logical question is, what type of support is best for each plant? Here is a quick guide to the main types I use in my container garden, and what I use them for.

STAKES

If you want to provide effective support, the main thing is to match the support to the ultimate size of the plant. Read the seed packet: if a tomato is going to be 170 cm/5½ feet tall, a 60-cm/ 2-foot stake is not much use. It can be very hard to believe that the tiny little seedlings you're planting are going to grow into such giants, but believe me, they will. And you do not want to be messing around changing the stake later on, as

you are likely to damage the plant and its roots. As a general rule, the stake should be about two-thirds of the final size of the plant.

Insert a sturdy stake – I use chestnut stakes for my tomatoes, and a solid piece of bamboo for plants such as kale or broad beans – next to each plant as you plant them out. Always put the stake with its back to the prevailing wind so that the plant will be blown away from the stake rather than onto it. Use garden twine to attach the plant to the stake, looping it around the stem under a set of leaves. Do this again at intervals as the plant grows taller. There is no need to mummify it – just add another tie when it has put on enough new growth to be looking vulnerable again. Give it enough slack to move a little in the breeze, but make sure the plant is held firmly enough for the stake to do its job.

More permanent plants, such as fruit trees, will need support too. Again, make sure you put the stake in place when you plant. Some sources recommend double or even triple staking, but I have always found that one is enough. You want the tree to be held so that its roots are stable and always in contact with the soil, but not held so rigidly that it snaps in a strong gust.

Choose a sturdy stake, tall enough that it comes to about half the height of the tree you are planting once you have pushed it into the soil. Position it towards the prevailing wind so that the tree is blown away from the stake rather than onto it, which could damage the trunk. I tie the tree to the stake using tarred twine. There are longer-lasting options, such as rubber tree ties, but my feeling is that you should be checking on the tree regularly anyway. If the tie breaks, it will prompt you to go in and do a bit of maintenance.

TRELLIS

Trellis is extremely useful in a small area, as it is a great way of opening up vertical space. You can buy ready-made sections of trellis in garden centres, or make your own; I like to use split chestnut stakes, as they are good and solid, but not too neat and square. You can attach

Supporting Plants

trellis to the wall, or simply to a couple of sturdy canes pushed down into your pots. Use it for climbing, twining plants, such as beans, peas and nasturtiums. Tomatoes and trained fruit trees will need tying in to the trellis at intervals to keep them secure. For my own trained trees, I have had to use freestanding supports as I cannot drill into our ancient brick walls. Mine are just simple chestnut frames pushed very firmly into the pot at the time of planting.

PEA STICKS AND BRUSHWOOD

While peas can grow up a trellis, they will be happier with something a little denser that gives their tendrils something to grab. Pea sticks or brushwood – short branches of plants such as hazel and birch, with all the fine twigs left on them – are perfect supports. Sweet peas love pea sticks too. You will often find them at good nurseries and garden centres, but if you're lucky enough to have a friend with a garden in the

country, just ask for some offcuts next time you're visiting. Make sure your pea sticks are at least as tall as the ultimate height of your plants, and push them well into the soil before adding your seeds or seedlings.

WIRES

If you are growing trained fruit trees – espaliered, cordon or fan (see page 231) – one of the neatest and least obtrusive ways to support them is to drill into the wall and insert vine eyes or nails so that you can create a framework of horizontal wires. The first one should be level with your first horizontal branches. Add more wires as needed at about 20-cm/8-inch intervals.

WIGWAMS AND OBELISKS

These freestanding structures, typically made from woven willow, hazel or metal, are very useful if you want to grow tall crops but don't have any walls to help support them. They also add height and visual interest to the container garden. Just make sure your wigwam is an appropriate height and strong enough to support the plant in question. I use an old metal salmon net for my climbing beans (opposite), and it works beautifully.

OTHER SUPPORTIVE IDEAS

Climbers, such as peas, beans and sweet peas, will be happy curling their way up a piece of twine. The twine will need to be attached to a support at the top, such as a gutter or a good strong nail in a wall, and can then simply be tied around the base of the plant, just under the first set of leaves. Always make sure the support you choose is strong enough to bear the weight of the crop. If you are going to bang a nail into a wall, try to put it in a place where you will be happy to have that crop every year, so you can reuse it.

Garden mesh can also be used to support climbers: just stretch it between two canes, making sure it is thick enough and the tension sufficient, to take the weight of the plants.

Finally, remember to make use of what you've already got. Many plants will be happy to scramble their way up a balustrade, or along the metal railings of a fence or balcony, creating a beautiful feature in the process.

Supporting Plants

PROTECTING PLANTS

My motto in the garden is, 'Never forget we are at war.' Whether it is slugs, birds or an unexpected frost, it can sometimes feel like we vegetable gardeners are under constant attack. It pays to be prepared. Physical barriers, such as fleece (see page 231), hessian (burlap), bubble wrap and netting, are cheap to buy, simple to use and will make an enormous difference to the success of your container garden.

A layer of fleece thrown over carrot seedlings is an effective way of keeping carrot fly at bay, but do remember that the fleece itself may harbour slugs and snails. I use netting too – a large mesh to keep birds away from fruit, and a finer one to frustrate the cabbage white butterflies, whose caterpillars will otherwise make doilies of your brassicas. Place canes around the edge of the pot and drape the netting or fleece over these, making sure birds can't get underneath. See page 233 for more on how to deal with these and other common pests.

The other main use for physical protection in the container garden is to guard against cold. If you are aiming to have crops throughout the year, or your container garden includes evergreen plants, this is something you will have to consider. Protection can also help you to extend the growing season by providing an insurance policy for early-sown crops. This is one of those situations where you will need to balance aesthetics with practicality. While you will not want to gaze out at a sea of bubble wrap or fleece, neither will you get any pleasure from looking at a lot of dead plants.

The simplest way to protect most crops is to cover them with a material such as fleece or hessian. The choice will depend on the climate: if you live somewhere sufficiently cold that plants need to be covered for lengthy periods of time, go for something that stops the heat escaping and lets light in. Bubble wrap is ideal, or you can use plastic or even glass cloches. If your plants need just a very temporary covering, you can use anything, from plastic sheeting to old net curtains. When a frost is forecast, put a few canes around the edge of the pot and drape your covering over the top. This method will also work well for larger plants, such as bay trees.

If the protection is going to be in place for a while, you will need to provide some ventilation, certainly in the UK, where damp is more of a threat than cold. If you are simply putting a layer of fleece over your pots or using cloches, lift them off during the day to let the air circulate. If you are protecting, say, a shrub or tree, you could protect just the side that's exposed to the prevailing wind, or maybe the top two-thirds of the plant. The top is the most vulnerable part, so covering only that allows air to flow up from the bottom.

THE DRAWBACKS OF PROTECTION

Do remember when covering plants that rodents will be looking for cosy places to overwinter, so make sure you are not inadvertently providing them with a home. When times are hard and food is short, they are quite likely to repay you for your hospitality by chomping their way through the roots of your precious plants.

On the whole, it is better to try to protect plants outside than to take them indoors. Most modern houses are simply too warm and dry for the majority of plants. If you really have no choice, try not to leave the plants inside for any longer than strictly necessary, or they will get soft, both literally and metaphorically, and may lose their dormancy.

The tougher your plants, the healthier and less disease-prone they will be. Really, the key is to work out how much they can stand and get them used to tough conditions. For example, if an autumn frost is forecast, don't bring them in – leave them out with light protection over them. That way they will be better prepared for whatever the winter brings.

Protecting Plants

The Container Kitchen Garden

HARVESTING

When it comes to harvesting, you must plan ahead. All your hard work will go to waste if you are not going to be around to pick the results. In most container gardens, it's extremely unlikely that you will have bumper crops to deal with, but it would still be upsetting to return from a trip and find that your prize apricots have rotted on the tree or that the birds got to them before you did.

Generally, from mid-summer through to autumn is likely to be your peak harvesting period. But of course it depends when you sow or plant, what varieties you choose, what the weather is like … there are so many variables. With practice, you will get better at predicting when things are going to be ready. If you know you will be away just as a crop is reaching its peak, do your best to draft someone in to pick it for you, even if that means giving it away. Better that than having it go to waste.

FREQUENCY OF PICKING

For some crops, regular harvesting is essential to keep plants productive and healthy. With peas and courgettes (zucchini), for example, the more you pick, the more you will get. Regular picking will help stop leafy plants such as Swiss chard getting congested, and keep the air circulating, which will ward off mildew. If you have multiple chard plants in a pot, remember to harvest from the middle as well as around the edges to open things up, and always cut the leaves from as close to the base as possible.

The same is true of cut-and-come-again salad leaves (greens). The key is to avoid disturbing the growing point – typically, the very centre of the plant. As long as you leave this growing point intact, the plant will continue to produce fresh new leaves. I reach in with my scissors or secateurs (pruning shears) and cut neatly, close to the base. If you're cooking for a crowd and need to take a lot of leaves, give the plants a good watering and feed afterwards to encourage new growth (see page 43). This is also a good time to top-dress the plants (see page 44) with, say, worm compost (see page 29).

With herbs such as coriander (cilantro) that are prone to running to seed, the trick is to keep harvesting the top leafy parts. Leave the base of the plants alone.

With container gardening in particular, the message is, use it or lose it. Plants grown in pots are more vulnerable to drying out and running to seed than those grown in a garden. Don't wait for that to happen. And don't make the mistake of waiting for a big harvest, either. Even if you have only a handful of something, enjoy it while it's at its best. Throw a few fresh peas into a salad, add a perfect tomato to an egg sandwich, make a single jar of apple compote, or even a bottle of blackcurrant vodka. Celebrate your produce when it is at its peak.

SAVING SEED

With the exception of coriander and dill seeds, both of which I use in the kitchen (see page 98), I tend not to save much seed from the container garden for the simple reason that I prefer to eat my crops rather than preserve them. Having said that, I do sometimes save some seed from more unusual varieties of vegetables, such as 'Australian Butter' climbing beans (see page 77), especially if I am not sure I will be able to get hold of the seeds again.

When you see the seed heads starting to brown, cut them off and lay them on newspaper on a sunny windowsill. The secret to saving seed is to make sure the seeds are properly dry before you store them, otherwise they will rot. Once the seeds are dry, transfer them to a jar, paper bag or envelope, and store somewhere cool and dry, away from direct light and – particularly if you are using paper bags – rodents. Don't forget to label the seeds.

Seed viability varies – sometimes (as with parsnips, for example) freshness is critical, sometimes less so – but generally I would try to use any saved seed within a year.

PRUNING & TRAINING

All fruit trees and bushes need regular pruning if they are to stay healthy and productive. Much is written about pruning, and it can be intimidating if you are just starting out, but it need not be difficult if you remember a few simple principles.

PRUNING AND TRAINING TREES

The main pruning of any tree, whether it is freestanding or trained against a wall, should take place in winter while the plant is dormant and the lack of leaves makes it easier to see the structure. The aim is to reduce congestion, encourage the tree to produce more fruiting wood, and maintain a good shape.

The first step is to take out any damaged wood, branches that rub against each other and weak growth. Next, cut back last year's growth on each main branch by about one-third. Always use sharp, clean secateurs (pruning shears) and cut back to an outward-facing bud. Get as close to the bud as you can without damaging it. Leave young side shoots unpruned so that they can develop fruit buds in the second year, but do remove any that are crossing or congested.

With freestanding trees, you should remove any branches that are growing into and obstructing the centre of the tree. The aim is to create an open 'goblet' shape so that air can circulate and you can easily access the fruit.

If you are growing a trained fruit tree, either as a single-stemmed cordon, fan or espalier (see page 231), winter pruning is your opportunity to direct the shape of the tree. Note that apricots should be pruned in summer, not winter, because they are vulnerable to silver leaf, a fungal disease that is most prevalent in autumn and winter.

If you have planted or purchased a maiden whip – a tree that consists of just a single stem – cut it back to the point where you want your first horizontal branches to appear. When they do, tie them into the support. Repeat as the tree grows and more horizontals appear, leaving about 20 cm/8 inches between each set and removing any shoots that are growing in the wrong place. With a feathered maiden – a single stem plus a few side shoots that have already grown – the principle is the same, although you will not need to cut it back when you first plant it. Just get rid of any side shoots that you don't want.

Trained trees will also need pruning during the summer, the aim being to reduce the new growth and to let in light and sunshine so that the fruit can ripen. It is also another good opportunity to correct and maintain the shape of the tree. Cut back new growth that is longer than about 20 cm/8 inches to five leaves, again cutting as close to the growth point as you can without damaging it. Remove all upright growth completely, as this interferes with the shape of the tree and will cause it to become congested. You can also look again for any crossing or diseased wood, and take it out.

PRUNING AND TRAINING BUSHES

With bushes, the pruning regime depends on the type of fruit, although the general principles – removing dead and diseased wood, ensuring good air circulation and encouraging fruiting – are the same as with trees.

Currants will need pruning in the winter. With blackcurrants and white currants you need to take whole branches down to the ground. Aim for a vase shape, open in the middle, and focus on removing the oldest branches first. With redcurrants, you should cut back new growth to about five buds and take out any old or congested wood at the base.

While most bushes need only one annual pruning, gooseberries need pruning in both winter and summer. During the winter, take out dead or old wood and cut back new growth to leave three sets of buds. During the summer, bring the new growth back under control and reduce congestion by cutting the side shoots back to five leaves once fruiting has finished. It will feel like you are being brutal, but you will be glad of it the following season when you are better able to reach the fruit. The aim is always to maintain an open 'goblet' shape, to encourage air circulation and make the fruit easier to pick.

Pruning & Training

POTTING ON SHRUBS & FRUIT TREES

Shrubs and trees grown in pots are at risk of running out of nutrients, so regular feeding is essential. However, you should also be prepared to repot them regularly. If the container size is generous, you won't need to do this every year, but you will need to be diligent about feeding and top-dressing (see page 44).

The general appearance and health of a plant is the best indicator of when it needs repotting. If the leaves are yellowing or smaller than they should be, or the fruit is forming late or not at all, you need to act. Keep a close eye out in early spring, as the new growth is a good indicator of general plant health. Look for decent-size leaves, and check the colour. If the leaves are usually dark green and they start to look yellow, it's time to repot.

To repot, tip the shrub or tree out of its pot. This may take a bit of negotiation, especially if it has been in there for a while. Try wiggling a trowel round the edge to loosen the compost (potting soil), then tip the pot and plant on its side and push up through the drainage holes at the bottom. With your hands, remove some of the old compost from around the trunk and roots.

This is also an opportunity to trim the roots. Get rid of anything dead or damaged and any big old gnarled roots. This will help to restrict the size of the plant, and also keep it fresh by encouraging new roots to form. If you are using the same pot, check that the drainage hole is still functioning, and brush out the pot to get rid of any remaining old compost.

Put some broken crockery or chunks of broken pot into the bottom of the pot you are going to pot into, followed by some compost, then put the plant into the pot. Push fresh compost around the sides of the pot – you don't need to pack it down, but make sure there are no air pockets as this will check the growth of the roots. The next step is to put fresh compost around the trunk or stems, making sure the plant is covered to the same level as it was before. Add a handful or two of plant food, such as blood, fish and bone meal (see page 231), then water well.

Generally, I try to put shrubs and trees into their 'forever' pots from the start, and keep repotting them into the same containers. You can use the space around the trunk or stems to grow other crops, such as salad leaves (greens) or herbs. If you are concerned that your plant might be outgrowing its pot, it's worth remembering that the size of the root ball is about the same as the top part of the plant.

When your shrubs and trees are very well established, you might get to the point where it is no longer practical to take them out of the pot altogether. In this situation, you can still refresh and rejuvenate them by scraping off the top layer of soil, trimming any exposed roots as you go, then topping up with fresh compost and feeding well.

Growing Guide

SALAD CROPS

SALAD LEAVES (GREENS)

I love to sow packets of mixed salad seeds; they are perfect for a shallow trough or pot, where the combination of different varieties can be displayed to great effect. There are so many combinations available now that choosing is just a case of experimenting and finding something you like for both flavour and appearance. Look for a packet that contains a wide range of varieties – chicory, mustard, rocket (arugula) and even Asian greens, such as mizuna, pak choi or tatsoi – to give you the maximum possible flavour and visual interest. The brilliant thing about these annual salad leaves is that the more you pick, the more they will grow – just pinch out individual leaves as close to the base of the plant as you can. Regular picking will also help keep the crops healthy by allowing air to circulate. Remember to water every day.

FAVOURITE VARIETIES

Seed companies seem to offer more and better different mixes every year. I am particularly fond of those that are tailored to the different seasons. In the UK, for example, crops such as mustard, rocket and mizuna are vulnerable to flea beetle (see page 233). I get round this by sowing mixes containing these varieties from mid-summer onwards. Early spring mixes will cope better with cold nights, as will plain old lettuce. Try mixing in some herbs to liven things up a bit.

KEY DATES

Sow salad leaves at about monthly intervals to ensure a continuous supply. Sow direct and as sparingly as you can. If the plants are congested, they will rot. If you find you've overdone it, just pull out some of the tiny seedlings and eat them, roots and all. Depending on the climate where you live, a late summer/early autumn sowing will keep going right through the winter. Each time you sow, do it into another pot – don't just add extra seeds to your existing crop, or it will get congested and the seedlings won't have space to grow.

COMMON PROBLEMS

Salad leaves are popular with slugs and snails, so use some organically approved slug pellets to get rid of these pests. The leaves can also be prone to mould, but regular picking will help to keep it at bay by allowing the air to circulate.

SORREL

It is well worth adding a pot of sorrel to your collection. With its distinctive flavour – sharply citrus and intensely green – just a little goes a very long way. It also needs to be eaten straight after picking, as it wilts very quickly. This is the reason you hardly ever see it in the shops. I love to add the young leaves to a salad in early spring, when fresh greens are in short supply, and I also enjoy making sorrel soup. The important thing with this crop is to keep picking and using it so that the leaves stay fresh and tender and it does not run to seed.

This is a perennial crop, so once it is established, there is little work beyond cutting it back a few times a year to refresh the plants, and keeping it well watered throughout the summer so it doesn't run to seed. In the growing season, it will need a good soaking every three or four days. Use a good-size pot – 30 cm/12 inches or so – as this plant has quite large, deep roots. When getting started, I suggest you buy young plants, rather than trying to grow them from seed, so that you have a good early crop.

FAVOURITE VARIETIES
Look for French sorrel, *Rumex scutatus*. Avoid the Russian variety – the flavour is not so good, and it is a much less elegant plant.

KEY DATES
Pot up young plants in early spring. Cut them back in autumn, adding leaf mould or compost to enrich the soil (see page 28), and do the same again in late spring. During the winter, lift and split the plants, enrich the soil and replant the healthiest-looking sections. Remember, you are looking to refresh the plants, not to start a sorrel farm, so don't replant it all. If you have more than you need, give some away.

COMMON PROBLEMS
The biggest challenge with sorrel is to stop it from running to seed. This is not a battle you are going to win, but cutting the plant back regularly will help to delay the inevitable. Watch out for slugs and snails too, especially when the young leaves start to emerge again after you've cut it back, and during the winter. I use organically approved slug pellets.

ROCKET (ARUGULA)

I found it much easier to grow rocket after I gave up thinking of it as a summer crop. In some climates you will fall foul of flea beetle (see page 233) if you sow the seeds early. Wait until after mid-summer and you will be rewarded with a wonderful salad crop that will see you through the autumn and, weather permitting, into the early winter. Cooler weather intensifies the flavour. Rocket is great for adding interest to salads, but it also makes wonderful pesto (see page 216). This annual plant is ideal for growing in a shallow pot or trough, as it is quick to mature and therefore does not need a great depth of soil. I water every other day to keep the leaves fresh and tender.

FAVOURITE VARIETIES
I like to grow 'Wild Rocket', which has smaller, more deeply cut leaves and a stronger peppery taste than other varieties. I also find it slower to run to seed than the larger-leaved forms.

KEY DATES
To my mind, there is little point sowing seed before mid-summer (see above), though in areas where flea beetles are not a problem on rocket, feel free to sow the seeds early in the season. Sow direct, where you want it to grow, and make sure the seedlings get plenty of water in the late summer heat.

COMMON PROBLEMS
Flea beetle is likely to be a problem with early sowings as the beetles thrive in dry conditions.

Growing Guide

FORCED CHICORY (BELGIAN ENDIVE)

For me, forced chicory (i.e. chicory that is artificially brought to maturity) is something that is synonymous with Great Dixter. It's a treat to enjoy the tender leaves of this annual out of season, and Christopher Lloyd loved to grow it. He would place the large pots on the stairs leading down to the billiard room in the basement. I love it as the basis for a winter salad, perhaps with some goat's cheese and nuts, or braised as a side dish to accompany roast meat or grilled (broiled) fish.

Forcing chicory is a slightly involved process, but good fun and well worth the effort. There is something quite magical about lifting the top of the forcer to find the pale chicons beneath. For forcing, you will need 'Witloof' chicory. Sow your seeds in small pots in the spring – they don't need to be under cover. Once you have decent strong seedlings about 5 cm/2 inches tall, prick them out (see page 35) into a larger pot, where they can continue to grow and develop strong roots. I am not going to dictate the size of the pot, as it will depend on how many plants you have or want to have, but remember that you will need to leave about 5 cm/2 inches between each plant. Your adolescent chicory plants will produce strappy leaves and may even flower. That's fine – just leave them to it. In the autumn, lift them, cut the tops off and pack the roots into a large, deep pot filled with a gritty compost (potting soil) mix. They can be very close together – all the goodness and energy they need for the winter is contained in the roots. Put a bucket over the top, making sure it blocks out all the light. The pots will then need to be kept somewhere frost-free, ideally in a shed or shelter of some kind. If you must keep them outside, wrap them very well in bubble wrap and hessian (burlap). It's vital that they are protected from frost. You should start to see buds, or chicons, emerge within a few weeks. When each bud is ready to harvest, cut it off at the base with a sharp knife. Each root will produce several buds, but they will be a little smaller each time. Eventually the root will run out of energy and can be discarded.

FAVOURITE VARIETIES
Look for the word 'Witloof', meaning 'white leaf', on the seed packet as this indicates varieties that are suitable for forcing.

KEY DATES
Sow seeds in early to mid-spring. Plant out the seedlings in late spring/early summer. In autumn, lift the roots, cut the tops off and repot the roots in a large container.

COMMON PROBLEMS
Watch out for slugs in autumn and winter when the buds are developing. With the damp UK climate and stone floors, Christopher had to use slug pellets even inside the house.

TOMATOES

Gardeners in the UK seem to take a particular pride in their tomatoes. Perhaps it is because, with our unreliable summers, it can be so hard to get those grown outdoors to ripen before they are struck down by blight (see page 231). Growing these annual plants in a pot can help

with this: not only are courtyards and other confined spaces often a little warmer than a garden, but the tomatoes can be moved around to catch the best of the heat and the sun. It is definitely worth trying. The smell and taste of a tomato, grown in real soil rather than hydroponically and ripened by the sun is beyond compare. If you do succeed, the best thing to do with your crop is as little as possible. Make a salad with mozzarella and basil, or dice and toss them (uncooked) through pasta with good olive oil. Of course, there is a place for roasted tomatoes too, not least in a tart.

To grow good tomatoes, sow the seed in early spring. You want to have decent-size plants by the time the frosts are over so that they are ready to make the most of the warm weather. Plant out into a large pot – I would put two into a pot around 45 cm/18 inches in diameter – and insert a strong stake at the back for support. As they grow, cut the leaves off the lower part of the plants to let in light and allow air to circulate, and pinch out the leaves that appear in the joints between the stem and the branches. Water every other day, and feed them too, with tomato food or liquid seaweed, right through the growing season. After that, all you have to do is pray for sunshine.

FAVOURITE VARIETIES
After years of experimentation, I have come to depend on 'Crimson Crush', which genuinely appears to be less susceptible to blight than other varieties. It produces a fairly large tomato that has an excellent flavour.

KEY DATES
Get the seeds started in early spring on a windowsill, and plant out once the frosts are over. Feed weekly throughout the growing season.

COMMON PROBLEMS
Blight (characterized by curling leaves with brown splodges on them, which then spread to the fruit too) is the big problem with tomatoes; once the plants have it, they're finished. It is a soil-borne disease, so start by using clean soil and be careful when you water so that soil isn't splashed up onto the tomatoes. Planting other things around

the base – try basil, creeping thyme or French marigolds (see pages 95, 102 or 109) – will also help with this, as will removing the lower leaves of the tomato plants. If, despite your efforts, blight strikes, pick the fruit immediately, even if it is still green. You can ripen it on the windowsill, or use it to make green tomato chutney. Tomatoes are also vulnerable to blossom end rot (characterized by a dark round patch at the blossom end of the fruit) if not given sufficient water.

SPRING ONIONS (SCALLIONS)

Christopher Lloyd could never see the point of growing normal onions on our heavy soil, since they are so cheap and readily available in the shops, and I am inclined to agree. Spring onions are a different story. They are a wonderfully useful addition to salads, and add a subtle onion flavour to tarts and soups. These annual plants also look great in a pot – a relatively shallow one will do, as the roots do not go very deep – and the smell of them will help to keep carrot fly away if you happen to be growing carrots too. I water thoroughly every three days or so.

FAVOURITE VARIETIES

For me the choice has to be 'White Lisbon'.
This variety of spring onion is extremely reliable,
and will happily overwinter too.

KEY DATES

Direct sow the seeds into the pot once the soil has
started to warm up – around mid- to late spring.
Once they are 10 cm/4 inches or so tall, thin out
the seedlings to give the remaining onions room
to expand. Use the thinnings in the kitchen.

COMMON PROBLEMS

Spring onions will bolt if allowed to dry out.
They will also struggle if they are overcrowded,
so do be diligent about thinning them (see above).

CUCUMBERS

I would like to make it clear from the outset that
I do not eat cucumber. Like all the men in my
family, I find it impossible to digest. But strange
as it may seem, I do not let that stop me growing
these annual plants. They are such a good-
looking crop, adding height and presence to the
vegetable garden – and, of course, many of my
guests do enjoy eating them.

Given a warm spot and sturdy support from
pea sticks or trellis, cucumbers will grow very
happily in a pot; you could even grow one up
a fruit tree. Ardent cucumber fans can put two
or three next to each other to create a screen
– handy if you do not like your neighbours. As
the plants grow, you will need to keep pinching
out the male flowers (the ones without a tiny
fruit behind them). They are a waste of the
plant's energy, and will also turn the fruit bitter
and seedy. When harvesting, snip them off with
scissors or secateurs (pruning shears). If you try
just to pull the cucumbers off, you could pull the
whole plant down with them.

FAVOURITE VARIETIES

One variety that did particularly well for me
in 2018 was an unnamed experimental variety
from a US company called Row 7 Seeds. Ask for
number 7082. If you are into juicing, the best
variety to choose is 'Long White'. It has a thin

skin, so the whole cucumber can be pushed
through a juicer without the need for peeling.

KEY DATES

As cucumbers need plenty of time in the sun to
ripen, sow the seeds in early spring to ensure
that you have good-size plants – say, 10 cm/
4 inches or so in height – by the time the frosts
are over and they can go outside. Cucumbers
will need daily watering once the fruits start to
develop – after all, they are 96 per cent water –
and a dose of liquid feed every ten days or so.

COMMON PROBLEMS

Like all fleshy-stemmed plants, cucumbers can
be prone to rotting if overwatered. Limit your
watering to once every three or four days when
the plants are small, increasing the frequency as
they grow and the fruits start to form. Powdery
mildew (see page 232) can be a problem later
in the summer, but while it might make the plant
look less attractive, it will not affect the fruit.

Growing Guide

ROOT VEGETABLES

CARROTS

It was a lady who came to one of my vegetable talks who first told me about growing carrots in pots. She said that she did it to outwit the carrot fly, which operate at ground level, so if you grow your carrots higher up, they should escape. It works brilliantly. Another great advantage with container growing is that you can tailor the environment to the crop. Carrots like it gritty, so I add some sharp sand to the mix – about one part sand to ten parts compost (potting soil). Tall, slender 'long Tom' pots are ideal. Being closer to the house, your carrots will be less exposed to the elements, and you can easily protect them on cold nights with a bit of hessian (burlap) (see page 50) to stop the soil freezing so that they are easy to harvest. I love carrots in all their different incarnations – slender, young and fresh in the summer, bigger and sweeter in the winter once the cold weather has started to turn the starches to sugar.

Carrots are best sown direct as they don't like root disturbance. You can buy special tape with the seeds correctly spaced out, but I prefer to sow from the packet, sprinkling them as thinly as I can. Inevitably, they will need to be thinned out further – initially to about 2.5 cm/ 1 inch apart, then even wider as the carrots grow bigger – but I look on this as a bonus. Each time you do it, you are rewarded with a handful of baby carrots to put in a salad, dip into hummus or enjoy just as they are. Water thoroughly twice a week for plump, tender roots. If you have never tasted home-grown carrots before, you are in for a treat.

FAVOURITE VARIETIES
'Early Nantes' has great flavour and I grow it successfully year after year. 'Danvers' is another good option, as it grows well in all soils, produces quite short carrots and has really good flavour. But perhaps the best all-rounder is 'Chantenay Red Cored', as it has excellent flavour, is so easy to grow and produces short, wide carrots.

KEY DATES
You can start sowing carrots in early to mid-spring and keep going right the way through to late summer to ensure a succession. Just keep popping more seeds into the spaces where you have harvested, or interplant them with other crops – remembering, of course, that they will need a tall pot to develop properly. Spring onions (scallions) would be the perfect partner, as the smell will keep carrot fly at bay. My preference is to sow carrots in late summer because the ensuing cold weather makes them sweeter, the carrot fly have flown away, and it is a wonderful crop to have when there is little else around.

COMMON PROBLEMS
Carrot fly is the number one problem. Using tall pots helps to keep them at bay, as does growing chives or spring onions (scallions) around the edge or nearby – carrot fly hate the strong smell. Carrots will also struggle in a soil that is too rich, or contains lumps of organic matter that haven't broken down. Use a good, soil-based compost and add some sand.

BEETROOT (BEET)

For me, beetroot is one of the greatest and most versatile of all vegetables. I love to use the greens as well as the roots. The young leaves are great in a salad, good simply boiled as a green vegetable, and delicious in a tart too. Even when the plants start to run to seed in the spring, they still make good eating, seeds and all. They will grow happily in a 30-cm/12-inch pot, will tolerate partial shade and their dramatic foliage will add a great deal of visual interest to your container garden, particularly if you interplant them with something contrasting, such as bright green lettuce. Have I said enough yet to convince you? If not, let me add that beetroot are very easy to grow provided you give the root enough space to develop. Remember, each one

POTATOES

The more I think about potatoes, the more I wonder why I bother to grow them in the vegetable garden at all. Growing them in a container makes it so much easier to earth them up – all you have to do is spread a bit more compost (potting soil) over the top, which really is the key to maximizing productivity. Potatoes will happily put out roots right the way up their stems, provided the stem is buried in compost.

If you have the space, grow potatoes in a 1-tonne bag, the type that suppliers use for bulk deliveries of compost or bark. Otherwise you can grow them in a bin (trashcan) or a sack. Just remember, each plant needs around 10 litres (9 quarts) of compost to grow in, so don't overcrowd them. Make sure the compost is good and rich too – this is a hungry crop – and water thoroughly every three or four days. As a guide, I am growing mine this year in sacks that are about knee-high. You can actually buy sets comprising a sack, seed potatoes, fertilizer and directions – a great way to get started. I half-filled the sacks with compost and pushed the potatoes in, leaving a good handspan-and-a-bit of space in between them. As they grow, I just add more compost on top, leaving a small amount of foliage exposed each time.

When the time comes, it's much easier to harvest potatoes in a container than in the ground, as you can simply up-end the whole thing and tip them out. No more heavy digging, only to come up with half a mangled potato on the end of your fork. And it is so rewarding too. There is very little that tastes better than a handful of salad (waxy) potatoes picked in the afternoon and on your plate that evening, tossed with a little sea salt, butter and mint. Potatoes will happily tolerate partial shade.

FAVOURITE VARIETIES

There are so many interesting potatoes available, including lots of heirloom varieties. Remember that early croppers – which tend to be the smaller, salad-type potatoes – will do particularly well in containers, and should also have finished doing their thing by the time blight (see page 231) hits. I must admit that I am a creature of

will ultimately be about the size of a tennis ball. You can sow direct, then thin them out as the young plants start to develop. Don't forget to eat the thinnings – they are delicious. One final plus: I have never found any need to feed them, provided they are in good soil-based compost (potting soil) (see page 28).

FAVOURITE VARIETIES

'Detroit', with its rich, deep flavour, retains its top position on my list of favourites. 'Boltardy' is a great choice for growing in pots, and lives up to its name, being noticeably slower to bolt than other varieties.

KEY DATES

Sow seed in early spring. Cover the pot with fleece (see page 231) to get the seed moving. If you have any leftover plants by the winter, they will also benefit from being covered if the weather turns very cold.

COMMON PROBLEMS

The only real problem you are likely to encounter is bolting, so be sure to give the plants plenty of water in warm, dry weather. A good soaking every three or four days should be enough.

habit, and always come back to 'Charlotte', which for me is the perfect salad potato. My friend Tom Coward says both 'International Kidney' (also known as Jersey Royals, provided they are grown in Jersey) and 'Wilja' have grown well in containers for him. 'Lady Christl' is another excellent old-fashioned variety, with great taste and texture.

KEY DATES

Start chitting (sprouting) potatoes in early spring. Put them on a windowsill – an empty egg box is the ideal container – and make sure they are getting plenty of light. Once they have formed strong shoots – no more than five or so per potato – get them into pots. You can do this earlier than you would in the garden, as the soil in a container will always be a few degrees warmer and it is much easier to cover them in case of a frost. Use something that lets the light through, such as hessian (burlap) or fleece (see page 231), and leave it in place for a couple of weeks after you've planted them, just to get them off to a good start.

COMMON PROBLEMS

Slugs love potatoes, so I use organically approved slug pellets to get rid of them. The main problem, though, is blight. This is an airborne fungal disease and once it takes hold there is little you can do about it. Getting started early will help, as blight tends to appear later on in the season. If you do see the telltale brown spots starting to appear on the leaves, remove the foliage immediately to stop the blight spreading down into the tubers. Don't put the blighted leaves on the compost – throw them away or burn them to stop the disease spreading. Since UK authorities deemed copper fungicides no longer suitable for organic gardening, I have not used anything to try to prevent blight. Just be observant and act quickly.

PARSNIPS

Parsnips always seem to me like a quintessentially English vegetable. While they may not have originated in England, they do seem to thrive here, and visitors from overseas are always keen to try them when they visit. My friends from Jerusalem, for example, can't grow them at all, as their soil is too poor and stony. Growing in a pot is an excellent way to avoid these problems and give them the conditions they need – namely, a good-quality compost (potting soil) free from stones or lumps of organic matter, and plenty of room to grow.

Like carrots, parsnips are best sown direct to avoid root disturbance. You must buy new seeds every year and make sure they are really fresh – look for a greenish tinge and a distinct parsnip smell. What I really like about them is the way you get two crops in one: the fresh young thinnings, tender enough to eat without peeling, and then later on the mature roots, roasted to caramel sweetness or adding body to winter soups and stews. Parsnips are another crop that will grow quite happily in partial shade.

FAVOURITE VARIETIES

'Countess' and 'Gladiator' are my tried-and-tested favourites, and always seem to perform well. Both of these can be eaten as young tender roots, or left to grow to standard size, when they will be delicious roasted, or in soups and stews.

KEY DATES
As parsnips are a crop that need plenty of time to reach a decent size before the winter and the all-important frost that turns their starches to sugar, sow them early in the spring. Cover with fleece (see page 231) to get them going.

COMMON PROBLEMS
The most common problem with parsnips is rust (see page 232). If you see the little reddish-brown spots on the leaves, pick the affected parsnip immediately – it should still be fine to eat – and burn or throw away the leaves. Don't add them to your compost bin, as this will encourage the rust to spread. Regular thinning out will help prevent it by encouraging better ventilation. Other than that, the main challenge will be to give the parsnips enough water – a thorough soaking every three or four days – so that they swell to a decent size and stay tender rather than becoming tough and woody.

LEEKS

Another great crop for a partially shaded spot, leeks will stand throughout the winter and make a fine focal point with their handsome foliage. There are some amazing colours available, from bright green to grey-blue and purple, so why not try a mixture for something really eye-catching? Leeks can be harvested at different stages of their growth, from tender young babies no thicker than your thumb to the heftier specimens of winter. And of course each time you thin them out, you are creating more space for the remaining vegetables to grow into.

I start my leek seeds off in a 12.5-cm/5-inch pot, then prick them out (see page 35) into their final position, leaving about 5 cm/2 inches between each plant. They will need a good-size pot, about 30 cm/12 inches in diameter, with plenty of depth. You can always thin them later if they need more space; the thinnings are absolutely delicious. Plant the seedlings good and deep, and fill the hole with water rather than

soil to help the roots settle in. Add some grit to the compost (potting soil) too – drainage is particularly important for winter crops.

I find leeks incredibly versatile and their flavour much less harsh than onions. Try them in a soup or tart, or simply cooked as a side dish.

FAVOURITE VARIETIES
'King Richard' is a great variety for growing in a pot, producing slender leeks that are ideal for harvesting young. I also like 'Musselburgh' for its great flavour and striking glaucous foliage. 'Megaton' is another excellent candidate, high-yielding and with good blue-green flags (sword-shaped leaves). Try a mix of them in the same pot for a really eye-catching display.

KEY DATES
Sow seeds in mid-spring. Once the seedlings are about half the thickness of a pencil, plant them out in their final position.

COMMON PROBLEMS

Leeks need regular, thorough watering every three or four days if they are not to bolt, but do be careful to avoid overwatering, which can make them slimy. They are also prone to rust (see page 232). It won't hurt you, but it will stop the leeks growing, so if you start to see rusty spots on the leaves, pull them up and eat them immediately.

RADISHES

Radishes are a brilliant container crop. Quick to mature and shallow-rooted, they are the perfect choice for a shallow container and also brilliant for tucking in among other crops – lettuce being the classic combination – to make efficient use of the space. Just pop a few seeds in between young seedlings, and by the time the main crop needs the space, the radishes will be in your kitchen, ready to be dipped into a dish of hummus while you are having a glass of wine and cooking supper. They're also good for adding crunch and colour to a salad, and I love them just sprinkled with a little sea salt. Try braising them too, as a side dish. Just heat a little butter and oil in a pan, add the radishes and stir,

then add a splash of stock (broth), wine or water and cook, covered, until they are soft. Cooking seems to mellow their pepperiness while leaving a pleasing touch of bitterness to their flavour.

FAVOURITE VARIETIES

'Scarlet Globe' is an excellent old-fashioned variety that always seems to do well, while 'French Breakfast', with its pink and white colouring, has a long, elegant shape and looks striking on the plate.

KEY DATES

Start sowing in early spring. As you harvest, pop more seeds into the gaps to make sure you have a supply right through the summer.

COMMON PROBLEMS

To do well, radishes require little more than rich, free-draining soil (no lumps) and plenty of water. I recommend watering every other day and thinning them regularly, as they will bolt if overcrowded.

Growing Guide

OTHER VEGETABLES

SWISS CHARD

When space is tight, you sometimes have to choose which vegetables are worth growing and which are not. Have no doubt – Swiss chard is definitely worth growing. For one thing, this annual plant is incredibly robust and crops the whole year round, making it amazing value for money. You can simply cut the leaves as you need them, and they will grow back. Another good reason for growing chard is that it wilts quite quickly after picking, so the leaves in the shops (if you can find them at all) tend to look rather sad. Then there is its beauty. With its shiny crinkled leaves and strikingly coloured, almost fluorescent stems, it makes an exotic adornment to any garden. Choose a big pot, as chard is a sturdy plant and vigorous grower, and water at least every other day to keep it looking lush. Of course, the main reason for growing it is that it is tasty and extremely useful in the kitchen: try it in tarts and soups, use the stems as an alternative to cauliflower in a cheese sauce, or serve it as a green leafy vegetable. The closely related perpetual spinach shares many of chard's attributes. While it is less glamorous, it is another brilliant year-round performer.

FAVOURITE VARIETIES
There seem to be new varieties of chard coming onto the market all the time. I'm currently enjoying a flirtation with 'Peppermint', which has wonderful pink and white striped stems like candy canes. But the one I come back to year after year is 'Flamingo'. The combination of cerise stems and deep green, shiny leaves is irresistible.

KEY DATES
Sow new seeds in spring, preferably before the previous year's crop runs to seed to ensure a continuous supply. I start mine either inside or under glass in a 10-cm/4-inch pot, then prick out the seedlings into their final position (see page 35). You can make life easier for yourself by sowing the seeds direct – just cover with some fleece (see page 231) to get them started. You will still get a good crop; it will just be a little later than if you were starting under cover.

COMMON PROBLEMS
While chard is generally hardy in the UK, it will suffer in a properly cold winter. In this case, cover it and move it to a sheltered spot. Apart from that, overcrowding is the main thing to look out for, as Swiss chard is rather prone to mildew and also very appealing to slugs and snails. The best way to offset these problems is to keep picking so that the plants can't grow too congested. Regular picking will also help to stop it from running to seed.

KALE

In recent years kale has become a 'fashionable' vegetable, widely promoted by health and fitness enthusiasts. In fact, people with good sense – and good taste – have been eating kale for years. Not only is it full of nutrients, it is also a reliable source of fresh greens when there is little else about. However, one thing that is new – and most welcome, in my view – is the proliferation of new varieties in all sorts of shapes and colours. These are perfect for adding interest to the container garden, especially in winter. Try planting a dark red or purple variety against the glaucous foliage of leeks, for example. Choose a generous pot, as this annual is a sturdy, long-lived vegetable, but not the thirstiest of crops; a good soaking twice a week will be enough.

I find kale incredibly useful in the kitchen, as an ingredient in a winter smoothie, a side dish or a healthy addition to soups, such as Oven-baked Lentil Soup with Greens (see page 136). It also makes the most brilliantly moreish kale crisps (chips). Just coarsely chop a handful of leaves, massage in some olive oil and salt, a squeeze of lemon juice and a little cayenne pepper if desired, then lay the leaves flat on a

position once they are about 5 cm/2 inches tall. Leave 10–15 cm/4–6 inches between the plants. The aim is to avoid the pests, but still give them a long enough growing season to reach a decent size before the cold weather hits and checks their growth.

Kale will happily survive most UK winters, but in a colder climate move pots to a sheltered position and use fleece (see page 231) for protection overnight, and even during the day if conditions are very harsh. Just remember to lift the fleece off when you can so air can circulate.

COMMON PROBLEMS
Pigeons can be a problem (see page 233), but are less likely to bother plants close to the house. Otherwise, the main enemy is the cabbage white butterfly. Try growing curly varieties to deter it, or cover the plants with a fine mesh (see page 50). I always prefer to use a physical barrier than resort to chemicals.

SEA KALE

Sea kale is a great choice for a container garden because you can give it the gritty, free-draining soil it needs to do well (remember, in the wild it grows in sand and shingle beaches). It also looks good, and, being hard to come by in the shops, is a conversation piece too.

I still remember the first time I tasted sea kale. My good friend Tom Coward, who is now the head gardener at Gravetye Manor in West Sussex, gave me a bunch for my birthday. Even grown 65 km/40 miles from the coast, it still tasted of the sea. Naturally, I ate it with fish – a truly magical combination.

Buy the small plants in spring – you can grow them from seed if you really want to, but you will be waiting a long time for your dinner – and plant them up. They have a very long taproot and do not like being disturbed, so put them into their 'forever' pot from the start. I use one about 35 cm/14 inches in diameter, and about the same in height. You will need to leave the plants to establish themselves for a season before you can start harvesting, but feed and water them in the meantime of course. The

baking sheet and bake in an oven preheated to 180°C/350°F/Gas Mark 4 for 10–15 minutes until crisp and lightly browned. Perfect with an aperitif while you are making the supper.

FAVOURITE VARIETIES
With so many varieties on the market now, it is difficult to choose, but I think my top three for their combination of flavour and colour would have to be 'Redbor', 'White Russian' – which is actually bright green with white ribs – and 'Red Russian'. 'Cavolo Nero' is beautiful too, with its deeply crinkled, nearly black leaves.

KEY DATES
I like to grow kale as a winter crop: the cold improves the flavour and also kills off the eggs of cabbage white butterflies, which can be a real nuisance when they hatch. I find the butterflies that do survive are less attracted to curly kale varieties, like the three I have selected. I start the seed off in pots in late spring or early summer, then prick them out (see page 35) into their final

edible part is the stems, and to make sure they are tender enough to eat you will need to force them (see page 231), just as you would with rhubarb. Once you start to see new growth in the spring, cover the pot with a forcer or bucket – anything that will block out the light and keep the slugs at bay. You can leave the forcer in place for a month or so while you are harvesting the stems. After this, remove the cover and leave the plant to shoot again. These exposed leaves will photosynthesize, enabling the plant to build up its strength for the next season.

FAVOURITE VARIETIES

The species sold by most nurseries is *Crambe maritima*, which is also the variety that occurs in the wild here in the UK. Fortunately, given that there is no choice, it is a winner: a sturdy mound-forming plant, with large glaucous leaves that make it a most attractive addition to the garden.

KEY DATES

Pot up young plants in spring, and leave them to grow for a full season before you start forcing them. Mulch the plants (see page 43) in the autumn to enrich the soil and protect them (see page 50) against the cold.

COMMON PROBLEMS

Sea kale needs good drainage to grow well, so make sure the soil is gritty and don't overwater – a good soaking once a week will do. Slugs love the young growth, so I use organically approved slug pellets to keep them away.

PEAS

Peas are a wonderful addition to the container garden. If you pick regularly, they will keep producing more pods, giving you a good yield from a relatively small space. They will also give your display a useful bit of height, and look really attractive scrambling up their twiggy support (see page 46). Just as with broad (fava) beans (see page 76), make sure the support goes in at the start – in this case, when you are sowing the seeds direct – so that you don't

damage the roots later on. You'll need pea sticks or brushwood to give the tendrils something to twine around. I like to put the sticks in the centre of the pot – make sure it's a large one, as this is a heavy crop – and sow the peas about 7.5–10 cm/3–4 inches apart around the edge so they are easy to access and get plenty of light. Peas are a wonderful example of an annual crop that tastes immeasurably better when eaten fresh, and the shoots are utterly delicious too, added to salads, pasta or risotto.

FAVOURITE VARIETIES
Christopher Lloyd's favourite variety – and the one we grow in the garden – is 'Hurst Green Shaft'. It does very well in a pot too. I also grow 'Sugar Ann', which, as the name suggests, is an exceptionally sweet pea. A new discovery this year is 'Dwarf Grey Sugar', an old variety of garnish pea with edible pods, flowers and shoots.

KEY DATES
Sow pea seed in early spring and put the pot in a warm spot. In early summer you can pull out any tired-looking plants and sow some fresh seed to get another crop. This second crop will need careful monitoring to make sure it gets enough water. If you are gardening in a hot climate, wait until autumn before sowing this second crop. Water thoroughly every other day to keep the peas fresh, plump and green.

COMMON PROBLEMS
Pigeons are the number one threat, with house sparrows a close second. Cover young plants with mesh or netting to keep them at bay (see page 50). Remove the protection once the peas have started to form in the pods.

BROAD (FAVA) BEANS

You will need a big pot to grow this annual crop, but once the broad beans get going and the pot is full, you will have a handsome-looking vegetable. As they grow, the plants tend to get rather leggy, so think about planting something else around the bottom. Violas would be perfect. Broad beans will also need support.

As always, this is best done before it is actually needed and ideally at the same time as you are planting up the pot. Put a couple of canes at the back, then loop twine around the sticks and the stems of the young plants, about 15 cm/6 inches from the ground. Eventually, you will end up with two or three layers of twine. Choose sticks that are about two-thirds the ultimate height of the beans (written on the seed packet) so that when the plants are mature, the sticks are completely hidden.

In the kitchen, broad beans make a wonderful addition to all sorts of dishes, including pasta, salads and couscous. The leafy tops (greens) make delicious eating too. Try wilting them in a little butter and stirring them into a risotto along with a few peas for a dish that is truly the essence of spring.

FAVOURITE VARIETIES
My current favourite is 'Crimson Flowered', which, as the name suggests, has the most beautiful

wine-red scented flowers. It is also particularly well suited to container growing because it's a compact plant.

KEY DATES

Broad bean seed can be sown direct in early spring, or the previous autumn for an earlier crop. They will keep growing slowly over the winter, then burst into life when the weather warms up. At least that is the theory. If you choose to go down this route, make sure you select a hardy variety. Should the weather be particularly chilly, cover with a cloche or fleece (see page 231) just to get them started. Remove it once the nights are a little warmer and the plants have really started to move. My personal preference is to sow in spring and have the beans a little later than go to the trouble of caring for the plants through the winter.

COMMON PROBLEMS

It is almost inevitable that black bean aphid will strike at some point. The later the crop, the more vulnerable it will be, which is a good reason to sow your beans in early spring. The aphids favour the leafy tops, so pinch those out and eat them as soon as your beans have reached their ultimate height.

CLIMBING BEANS

It was a pot of beans that first gave me the idea for this book (see page 12). A couple of summers ago I had some spare plants left over from the garden. Not wanting to waste them, I planted them in a large plastic pot and gave them a salmon net to climb up. It was a revelation. They tasted so fresh and delicious, and it was such a treat to be able to grab a handful from just outside the door as a last-minute addition to my supper.

Beans are well suited to growing in a confined space, as they enjoy the additional warmth and shelter from the elements. Like peas, these annual plants will add some useful height and drama to your display, and provide colour from their flowers and, with some varieties, the pods too. They will also need a large pot to support

all that top growth. For extra support, you can use tall pea sticks, brushwood, twine, trellis or canes, putting two plants at the base of each stick. Do make sure you can still reach the top, though. All beans are thirsty and will quickly become tough without sufficient moisture, so give them a thorough watering every other day.

French (snap) beans are great croppers and, if picked regularly, should keep you supplied right through the summer. I like a handful blanched and thrown into a salad, or just as a side dish, but they stand up well to more robust summer flavours.

FAVOURITE VARIETIES

My old standby is 'Cobra', but lately my head has been turned by a variety called 'Australian Butter'. With its yellow pods, it looks most attractive, and they are equally good eaten young, pods and all, or as podded (shelled) beans later in the season. 'Cosse Violette' is another colourful variety, with fabulous purple

flowers and pods. But perhaps most glamorous of all is the Italian borlotti (cranberry) bean 'Lingua di Fuoco', with its glorious speckled red and white pods. Unlike other climbing beans, borlotti pods are not edible, but the beans inside are delicious. Eat them fresh, or leave them to dry on the windowsill to enjoy in the winter.

KEY DATES
Sow seed direct from mid-spring, or once the night-time temperature is consistently above 7°C/45°F. If you start too early, the seeds will sit and sulk and may even rot.

COMMON PROBLEMS
Watch out for cold nights at the start of the growing season, and for strong winds, which can scorch the young plants. Use fleece (see page 231) or windbreak fabric for protection. Young beans are popular with slugs, so I sprinkle a few organically approved slug pellets over the pot. You will also need to be careful with watering in the early stages. Make sure your soil is free-draining so the plants aren't sitting in water. Up the watering once they are growing well to ensure a good supply of tender beans.

GLOBE ARTICHOKES

Globe artichokes arguably deserve their place in the container garden for their sheer beauty and architectural presence alone. The fact that they make good eating, too, is a bonus. Artichokes will need a large pot – 40 cm/16 inches in diameter – if they are to do well, and good, well-drained soil. However, they will do better if the plug plants are started off in a smaller pot, then moved on to their 'forever' pot once they are established. This is because they are prone to rotting and will not like being surrounded by surplus wet compost (potting soil). Give them a good soak every four days or so. Although perennial, the plants will need replacing every couple of years to keep them fresh and productive. Fortunately, they are very easy to propagate. Just take the plant out of the pot in early to mid-spring and, using a sharp knife, cut off slips (sections of the plant that include both shoot and root) from around the edge, where growth is strongest. Discard the rest, then repot the slips. They will produce artichokes in the same year, albeit somewhat later in the season. Having two pots will get round this problem by enabling you to refresh them one at a time in alternate years. In the kitchen, I do not think there is a better starter (appetizer) than an artichoke simply boiled and served with a good vinaigrette. For a fantastic side dish, try the recipe for Stuffed Artichokes (see page 148).

FAVOURITE VARIETIES
I grow 'Gros Camus de Bretagne' and 'Gros Vert de Laon'. Both are productive and hardy in the UK climate. They are also very easy to propagate.

KEY DATES
In the UK, mulching the plants in autumn (see page 43) should be sufficient to protect them over the winter. In colder climates, you may need to move the plants to a garage or cellar. If you don't have access to a sheltered spot, you can remove the plants from their pots altogether: cut back the top growth and store the roots, wrapped in moss or damp newspaper to keep them from drying out, in the refrigerator, then replant the roots in spring.

Take slips in spring, once the plants start to come back into growth. This is also the time to pot up new plants.

COMMON PROBLEMS
Artichokes are good-tempered plants, but do make sure they get enough water and are in a sunny position. The only major problem you are likely to encounter is blackfly on the buds. I have to say, I am pretty lazy when it comes to dealing with pests, and don't usually take any action beyond washing the artichokes carefully before cooking them. However, giving the growing plants a squirt of soapy water will help to keep the invaders down.

FENNEL

After years of trial and error, I have found that the key to growing fennel successfully is to avoid planting in high summer because it bolts very easily. Start it off a bit later and you will have the most fantastic autumn crop, with wonderful foliage to enjoy for both its looks and flavour in the meantime. Try adding a finely chopped handful to a potato salad, or stir into mayonnaise to eat alongside fish.

Fennel will need a reasonable amount of space to grow if it is to develop a decent-size bulb – I have three growing in a 30-cm/12-inch pot – but if you find you have overplanted, you can always eat the thinnings too, just as with carrots and beetroot (beet) (see page 67). If you are interplanting with another crop – say, lettuces – make sure you leave enough space for the fennel to grow without being smothered. And be careful not to accidentally weed it out. Daily watering is vital too. This annual vegetable has such a distinctive flavour that a little goes a long way: a single good bulb is enough to enhance a salad for six. If you do decide to sow early, you can also let some of the plants run to seed. Sprinkle the flowers over a salad or fish carpaccio, and use the seeds either as a flavouring or to save for your next year's crop.

FAVOURITE VARIETIES
I chose 'Victoria' initially because I liked the name, but a few years on I can report that it has

well and truly earned its place at Great Dixter because it doesn't bolt, forms good plump bulbs and has excellent flavour. I have also found that 'F1 Rondo' and 'Zefa Fino' are less prone to bolting than some other varieties.

KEY DATES
Sow the seed in early spring or wait until late summer, as fennel is very vulnerable to bolting in mid-summer. Prick out the seedlings into their 'forever' pot once they are about 5 cm/2 inches tall (see page 35). Note that an early sowing will need some protection from the elements in order to get going (see page 50). Alternatively, you could sow direct, in which case you will have to be a little more diligent about thinning out.

COMMON PROBLEMS
Bolting is the biggest problem you are likely to encounter. Direct sowing can help with this because transplanting causes stress, and a stressed plant is more likely to bolt.

COURGETTES (ZUCCHINI)

Courgettes make a wonderful container plant. They have architectural foliage, and they are very productive too, which is always heartening. These annual vegetables are also a great thing to grow if you want to introduce children to gardening because the seedlings are large enough to handle easily and they produce results very quickly. Take care, though; just one or two plants is ample, unless you have a vast family or an army of friends to feed.

Courgettes need plenty of space, so give each plant a decent-size pot – say, 35 cm/ 14 inches in diameter. If you want to put two plants together, you will need to leave 60 cm/ 2 feet between them, which probably means choosing a trough rather than a pot. They will need a good rich soil, a weekly feed throughout the growing season and plenty of water. A layer of mulch in the summer will help stop them drying out (see page 43).

Growing courgettes yourself means you can pick them young and small, when the flavour and texture are at their peak. I love them raw, grilled (broiled), sautéed, roasted ... you name it. They are brilliant with garlic, or a little lemon zest, and with herbs such as thyme and basil.

You can eat the courgette flowers too: look for the males, the ones that don't have a tiny fruit forming behind them. These are wonderful stuffed with soft cheese and fried in olive oil. Be careful not to take all the flowers, though – you need to leave some to ensure pollination and keep the fruit coming.

FAVOURITE VARIETIES
Bright yellow 'Cube of Butter' grows well in a container and adds a jolt of colour to the pot display. 'Tiger Cross', with its green and white stripes, is another great choice. For traditionalists, though, it is hard to beat 'Dunja', with its glossy, dark green fruits, for flavour and productivity.

KEY DATES
Sow courgette seed in mid- to late spring. It will need a bit of warmth and sun to germinate – a windowsill is perfect. I put four or five seeds in a 10-cm/4-inch pot, then prick them out (see page

35). The seedlings do grow very quickly, so keep an eye on them to make sure they're still looking healthy and not outgrowing the pot. You will need to wait until after the frosts are finished before planting them out, so you might need to move them into a slightly larger pot with some fresh compost (potting soil) in the meantime. The key thing is to keep the courgette plants growing.

COMMON PROBLEMS

Getting the balance right with watering can be tricky. Courgettes are prone to rotting when young, so you will need to be careful not to overdo it. As the plants mature and the courgettes start to form, regular, generous watering (daily, if possible) is essential to avoid blossom end rot. This occurs when lack of water means plants can't take up sufficient calcium from the soil. Courgettes are also susceptible to mildew, although this will affect the leaves rather than the fruit. Removing older leaves will help to improve air circulation and also give the sun a chance to get to the fruit and ripen it. Finally, a sprinkling of organically approved slug pellets never goes amiss.

BUTTERNUT SQUASH

I recently grew my first butternut squash in a pot and it was both fun and a great success. It is great that seed companies are starting to offer varieties specifically suited to growing well in pots; lack of space no longer needs to be a barrier to growing what you want.

Squashes need a decent spell of warm weather to ripen properly – essential if you are planning to store them for any length of time – so you want to sow this annual crop early with the aim of having good-size plants ready to go out as soon as the frosts are over to maximize their exposure to the heat. You may well find that home-grown squashes keep better than shop-bought ones. That's because commercial crops get a lot of water, which tends to result in bigger fruit but thinner, more easily damaged skin. Of course, your squash in a pot will need regular watering too, as well as feeding – this

is a hungry crop, and will benefit from a good rich soil with some extra organic matter added to it (see page 44). I love to eat squash simply roasted or mashed, the perfect accompaniment to sausages. Otherwise it makes a wonderful velvety soup, and is fantastic for stuffing with spiced minced (ground) beef (see page 142).

FAVOURITE VARIETIES

Most recently, I grew two varieties, 'Butterbush' and 'Barbara', that have been specially bred for growing in containers. Both performed well, but 'Butterbush' was the most productive, and the one I am likely to grow again. Next year I may try getting it to grow up a trellis on a sunny wall. For obvious reasons, it is probably a good idea to avoid any varieties with 'Giant' in their name.

KEY DATES

Sow the seed in early spring and keep the pots on a warm windowsill. Plant out once the frosts are over and the plants have reached a decent size, with a couple of sets of true leaves (see page 35). They will need the whole summer to mature. Feed weekly once they start to set fruit.

COMMON PROBLEMS

Given half a chance, slugs will nibble right around the stems of young plants, so I use organically approved slug pellets to fend them off. Also, do be careful not to overwater: young plants are prone to rotting if they are too wet, and excessive water later on will result in thin-skinned squashes that will not store well. Water thoroughly every three or four days.

If you are lucky enough to have a good growing season and produce some large fruits, you may find that the individual fruits themselves need support if they are not to drop off the plant before ripening. The best way to do this is by making a small sling or hammock to support the fruit – nylon stockings are ideal. The ends will need to be tied to a firm support or trellis.

AUBERGINES (EGGPLANTS)

If you really want to impress, grow an aubergine. It is not the easiest thing to do, especially in a country like the UK where the summers are unreliable, but at least if you have it in a pot, you can keep moving it around to catch the sun. Buy young plants, rather than trying to grow them from seed. This will reduce your choice of varieties, but increase your chances of success. Pot it into your own compost (potting soil) as soon as you get it home. Choose a large pot (at least 40 cm/16 inches across) and put a decent stake in before planting out: if the plant thrives and produces fruit, it's going to need a sturdy support. Find a sunny spot for it on a windowsill until the cold nights are finished and it can go outside. Once the fruit is setting, start feeding the plant weekly with a good liquid feed.

Aubergines are useful in the kitchen. I love them roasted, grilled (broiled) or, better still, barbecued, which gives them a wonderful smoky flavour. Try them in a char-grilled summer vegetable salad with tomatoes and courgettes (zucchini), or coarsely blended as a dip.

FAVOURITE VARIETIES

My advice here is to be pragmatic and grow whatever variety is available from your local garden centre or nursery. In the UK at least, aubergine is not a widely grown annual crop, so choice is limited. If you do decide you want to take the challenge one step further and grow an aubergine from seed, choose one that is suited to your climate. Either way, you are only likely to achieve success if you have a good sheltered spot and plenty of sun. If the plants are struggling outside, a bright porch or windowsill is a good alternative.

KEY DATES

If sowing seeds, do so in early spring. Put them on a sunny windowsill to get them started. The aim is to have a good, strong plant ready to put outside when the weather has warmed up.

COMMON PROBLEMS

Overwatering when plants are small will cause them to rot, so go carefully. Once the fruit is setting, start to increase the watering to about every three or four days. Plants grown inside will be susceptible to greenfly (see page 233) and

red spider mite. Fresh air is the best antidote. In some areas, flea beetle (see page 233) can be a problem. The best solution is a simple physical barrier: cover pots and young plants with fleece (see page 231).

CHILLIES

I do not grow chillies for gastronomic pleasure. I know I have said elsewhere that you should grow what you want to eat, but there is always room for an exception, especially when it is as colourful and eye-catching as chillies. They add so much interest to a display, and I am always happy to have something to give away to friends. They are also incredibly easy to grow. This is a Mediterranean crop and well used to tough conditions. Just give the plants some sun, and possibly a small stake for extra support if they are in a windy spot (see page 46). If you start with good soil-based compost (potting soil), you won't even need to feed them. Most chilli plants can be treated as perennials, though they will need to be brought inside or protected with fleece (see page 231) over the winter. A word of advice if you are growing them to eat, rather than just for show: the capsaicin that gives the fruit its heat is not soluble in water, so if you find that you have bitten off more than your pain threshold allows, reach for a glass of milk to cool things down.

FAVOURITE VARIETIES

I tend to buy my chillies as small plants from the garden centre and usually look for jalapeño types, as they are medium-hot and very productive. 'Summer Heat' has beautiful scarlet fruit that grow sweeter as they get riper. I also like 'Giant Jalapeño', which, as the name suggests, produces extra-long peppers that can be eaten either green or red, and are not too eye-wateringly hot. Use green jalapeños in salsa and sauces, and dry them when red to keep you in chillies throughout the year. If you are growing from seed, try 'Cherry Bomb', with its sweet little, round red chillies, rather like tiny apples. 'Twilight' is another excellent variety, which has purple, yellow, orange and red chillies all showing at the same time.

KEY DATES

If you are growing from seed rather than buying small plants, start in early spring so that you have good strong plants ready to go out as soon as the frosts are over. They will need maximum exposure to sunlight if they are to ripen. Water every three or four days throughout the growing season. If you are overwintering chilli plants, cut the old growth back in late winter/early spring to encourage new shoots to appear.

COMMON PROBLEMS

In the early stages, while plants are still being grown under cover, they may be prone to whitefly (see page 233). The best cure is a dose of fresh air, so put them outside whenever the weather permits. Other than this, the only real challenge for those of us gardening in temperate climates is getting them to ripen. Be prepared to move the pot around to catch as much sun as possible.

Growing Guide

FRUIT

ALPINE STRAWBERRIES

I will never forget the first time I tasted Alpine strawberries, in a market in Switzerland. These tiny fruits are miniature flavour bombs, smelling and tasting of vanilla and violets. Try putting these perennial plants around the base of a fruit tree, or let them fill a shallow trough or planter. The only real problem is that, because the strawberries are so tiny, you will need a lot of plants if you plan to share the fruit. I get around that problem by keeping them all for myself. There is nothing better than eating them straight from the plant on a sunny afternoon, although I must admit a shot glass of frozen strawberry vodka (see Fruit Vodka, page 228) comes a close second. Whatever you intend to do with them, wait until they are dark red before you pick them for the most intense flavour.

FAVOURITE VARIETIES
These precious little fruits can go by many different names, including wild or woodland strawberries. *Fragaria vesca* is the Latin name to look out for, as opposed to *Fragaria × ananassa*, which is the larger garden strawberry.

KEY DATES
Buy new plants in the spring. If you are putting them around the base of a tree, watch carefully to make sure they are getting enough water in the summer. A good soaking once a week should be sufficient. Like most plants, they will thank you for a top-dressing of organic matter (see page 44) at the start of the growing season. They should start fruiting in early summer, and will continue right into the autumn, provided the weather stays mild.

COMMON PROBLEMS
Slugs and snails can be a problem in spring, so invest in some organically approved slug pellets. Keep on top of the weeding too, while the plants are getting established. Once they are, though, you will have the opposite problem: thriving strawberry plants will form a mat of roots through which other things will struggle to grow. Keep an eye on this if you are combining them with other crops. They are also susceptible to grey mould, but thinning them from time to time will help prevent this and also tackle any congestion.

BLUEBERRIES

For me, blueberries alone are reason enough to have a container garden. These acid-loving plants struggle on our clay soil at Great Dixter, so by growing them in a pot I am able to control their environment and give them exactly what they need – in this case a 50:50 mix of John Innes soil-based compost (potting soil) and ericaceous (acidic) compost. I also water them with rainwater, as the lime in tap water will affect the pH of the soil over time. During the growing season, water them thoroughly once every three or four days. A weekly feed with

ericaceous plant food will help keep the balance right. They may need occasional watering in winter too, if the weather is particularly dry and mild. Look out for compact forms so that they don't get too top-heavy, and choose a good-size pot, about 40 cm/16 inches in diameter. Blueberries will need repotting every two years (see page 56).

FAVOURITE VARIETIES
'Top Hat' and 'Sunshine Blue' both perform well and are excellent croppers, with good-size fruit. They're also quite compact, so will thrive in a pot. 'Top Hat' has very ornamental flowers.

KEY DATES
In spring, top-dress (see page 44) blueberries with pine needles or crushed pine bark to add more acid to the soil. In winter, clean out any dead or damaged wood. Beyond this, blueberries do not need pruning.

COMMON PROBLEMS
The main challenge is to maintain the acidity of the soil. Other than that, blueberries are fairly trouble-free.

GOOSEBERRIES

I find the gooseberry bush particularly beautiful during the winter, when its ghost-like stems stand out against the gloom. This is something worth considering when you are going to be looking at it through your window for most of the year. Another advantage is that it will happily tolerate some shade. I also find it generous, essentially giving two crops for the price of one: picked early, the berries are a wonderfully sharp foil for cream in a simple fool (a dessert made by blending fruit purée with whipped cream); left to ripen fully, they can be as sweet and fragrant as a grape, particularly if you choose one of the newer varieties.

Pruning gooseberries is rather a challenge, as they are covered in vicious thorns, so make sure you are wearing thorn-proof gloves and long sleeves. You will appreciate having trimmed them into an open 'goblet' shape when it comes

to picking because it allows you to reach into the middle and access all the fruit. Like any long-lived plant, gooseberries need a large pot. Mine is about 40 cm/16 inches across.

FAVOURITE VARIETIES
If you have space for two bushes, I would go for 'Hinnonmaki Red' and 'Hinnonmaki Yellow'. Otherwise, just choose whichever colour you like best. These are great examples of modern cultivars that are sweet enough to eat raw when fully ripe.

KEY DATES
Plant new gooseberry bushes in the spring. Established plants will benefit from pruning in winter and summer (see page 54). Top-dress the plants in spring (see page 44), and use a potassium-rich fertilizer such as blood, fish and bone meal (see page 231), liquid seaweed or tomato food around the base of the plant and out to its circumference a couple of times during the season, once the fruit has started to set. Water well, particularly in early summer when the fruit is forming. A good soaking once a week will be enough, unless the weather is particularly warm, in which case you should do it every three

or four days. Check water levels in winter too, so that they don't dry out during mild weather.

COMMON PROBLEMS

Gooseberry sawfly can damage the leaves. As with all crops I'm going to eat, I prefer to pick off the small caterpillars from the underside rather than spray them, and to focus my efforts on keeping the plant well pruned, fed and watered.

CURRANTS

Redcurrants, white currants and blackcurrants are great choices for a partly shady spot, and their gem-like fruit is a striking feature in the summer. Currant bushes are undemanding plants – just give them a good soaking every three or four days. In winter, check on them during warm dry spells so that they don't dry out. For me, an added bonus is the smell of the blackcurrants, which I find delicious, although not everyone feels the same. They are also invaluable in the kitchen for custards, tarts, jellies and jams, or served just as they are with a scoop of ice-cream. And, of course, there is currant vodka too (see Fruit Vodka, page 228).

FAVOURITE VARIETIES

My favourite blackcurrant is 'Boskoop Giant', which produces thin-skinned fruit of luscious juiciness and excellent flavour. For redcurrants, I favour 'Jonkheer van Tets'. The large, sweet fruit is easy to pick and ripens early in the season. As for white currants, I find 'White Versailles' to be by far the best for flavour.

KEY DATES

Pot up new plants in spring to give them the best chance of getting established through the summer and autumn, before the colder weather returns. Choose a large pot around 40 cm/ 16 inches across. Established plants should be pruned in winter (see page 54). After pruning, mulch them around the base (see page 43). Start feeding in spring once new growth appears, and continue throughout the growing season.

COMMON PROBLEMS

Currants are pretty tolerant. Birds will be your only major concern, so cover the plants with netting when they are fruiting (see page 233).

APPLES

Apples are a great choice for the container garden. Trees grown on dwarfing rootstock (see page 231) will fruit sooner than standard trees, and are tolerant of partial shade, making them a little more flexible in terms of position than sun-loving figs and apricots. They will also grow happily flat against a wall, trained either as a fan or an espalier (see page 231). Another great innovation in the world of apple trees for patios and pots is the multi-variety tree, where more than one variety is grafted onto the same rootstock. This means you can have, say, dessert and cooking apples from the same tree – ideal in a small space – and extend the cropping season by choosing one variety that crops early and one that crops late. Whatever you choose, give the pot a good soak once a week, or every three to four days in warm weather. Like all container plants, apple trees can be prone to drying out in winter too. Keep an eye on them and water during mild, dry spells.

FAVOURITE VARIETIES

You will need to decide whether you're looking for cooking or eating apples, or hedge your bets with a single tree that offers both. I am growing two eaters: 'Red Falstaff', an excellent late-fruiting variety with a beautiful red skin, and 'Egremont Russet', which I love for its dry, nutty flavour.

KEY DATES

Plant new apple trees and top-dress established ones in the spring (see page 44). Spring is also the time to repot if you need to (see page 56). The bigger the pot you start with – mine is around 45 cm/18 inches in diameter – and the richer your soil, the longer your plant can be left. Apple trees will need pruning in both winter and summer (see page 54).

COMMON PROBLEMS

There is almost no end to the list of pests and diseases that affect apples: aphids, powdery mildew (see page 232), canker, apple scab …. There is plenty of good advice available on how to deal with all these things, but my attitude is quite relaxed; as long as the tree is producing edible fruit, I am not going to worry too much. Keeping the plant healthy and strong is the best defence. Prune regularly to get rid of any broken or diseased wood, be diligent about feeding and water thoroughly – twice a week in the summer (see pages 43, 44 and 54).

FIGS

I can still recall the taste of the wild figs that I once ate out in the Israeli desert. What struck me, apart from the amazing flavour, was just how little soil the plant needed to grow and be productive. This makes it ideal for small spaces, provided there is plenty of sun. Indeed, if I could have only one tree in my container garden, it would be a fig. The fruit is wonderful eaten just as it is, but try it grilled (broiled) with honey or in a salad with goat's cheese. Figs are very easy to train as a fan against the wall (see page 231), and do not demand much in the way of food and water. I fork in a bit of blood, fish and bone meal (see page 231) in spring and try

to give the pot a good soaking once a week. Despite coming from desert conditions, fig trees are tough in the cold too. In the UK, a fleece (see page 231) thrown over them when the temperature drops should suffice; in a colder climate, move the tree under cover if at all possible. Water when needed in the winter.

FAVOURITE VARIETIES

At Great Dixter we grow 'Brown Turkey' for its dense, richly flavoured fruit. Its figs are a bit smaller than usual, but they have a delicious flavour and the skin is good to eat too.

KEY DATES

Plant your fig tree in the early spring and prune during the winter. Figs fruit on old wood, so you need to prune for shape and the overall health of the tree rather than to encourage new growth. Take out whole branches down to the base.

COMMON PROBLEMS

While fig trees are generally undemanding, you will need to keep an eye on them during hot weather. Don't let them dry out, otherwise their leaves will tend to drop. Birds are big fans too, and may well get to the fruit before you do unless you fling some netting over the tree.

PEACHES

There are few things more impressive than a fan-trained peach (see page 231) with its soft pink blossom and luscious fruit. All you will need is a warm wall, plenty of sun and deep enough pockets to buy a large pot, around 45–50 cm/18–20 inches in diameter. Of course, untrained peach trees are a glorious sight too, but for those of us gardening in a temperate climate, fan-training is the better way to go, because of the additional heat reflected back from the wall, which helps the fruit to ripen. It's also an efficient way of using the space. Water once a week, or every three to four days in hot weather, soaking the pot thoroughly each time. In winter, it's worth checking the tree during mild dry spells to make sure it doesn't dry out. As the fruit starts to develop, thin it out so that

Fruit

Growing Guide

page 54). Peach blossom appears early in the season, so the tree may need protecting with fleece (see page 231) if the spring is very cold.

COMMON PROBLEMS

Peaches are susceptible to peach leaf curl, so will need to be sprayed with a copper- or sulphur-based fungicide in the autumn, after the leaves drop, and again in early spring, just before the buds start to form. You might also need to cover your tree when the fruit starts to mature in order to stop the birds reaching your precious fruit.

APRICOTS

An apricot tree is an investment, particularly if you are treating yourself to a mature plant that will crop sooner than a young one, so it is worth seeking out a good nursery for the best choice and expert advice. Make sure your tree is grafted onto dwarfing rootstock (see page 231) and that it is self-pollinating (see page 232): you don't want to wait years for your apricot to fruit only to find it is languishing for want of a lover. When your tree arrives, plant it straight into its 'forever' pot, which should be 45–50 cm/18–20 inches in diameter. Don't worry if the tree looks too small to start with; it will soon fill out. The space around the tree's base is ideal for Alpine strawberries (see page 85), a combination to make anyone swoon with joy. Give the plant a good soak once a week, or every three or four days if the weather is hot, and as needed throughout the winter. This is much more effective than more frequent, shallower watering.

the remaining peaches have space to flourish. Just pinch out any small or unhealthy-looking fruit, aiming to leave around 10 cm/4 inches between those remaining.

FAVOURITE VARIETIES

Dwarf forms are often sold unnamed. I have chosen 'Garden Lady', which is a slow-growing variety and therefore ideal for pots. It has beautiful pink blossom and is self-fertile. The fruit has delicious yellow flesh, and the stone is very easy to remove – a great attribute for a peach to have.

KEY DATES

Get your tree in early spring and plant it immediately. Feed every two weeks with a liquid feed throughout the growing season and top-dress with worm compost or organic matter every spring (see page 44). Repot every five years or so (see page 56). Fan-trained trees will need pruning in summer to maintain their shape, as well as in winter to control their growth (see

FAVOURITE VARIETIES

Look for a dwarf type – the key words to look for on the label are 'patio' and 'pot'. I have chosen 'Isabelle', which fruits late in the season, after mid-summer. This makes sense in a temperate climate, where the fruit will need all the heat the summer can offer in order to ripen.

KEY DATES

My preference would always be to buy a bare-root tree (see page 40) in the early spring.

Remember that you will need to deal with it as soon as it arrives, so have your pot and compost (potting soil) ready. A container-grown plant will be more forgiving, but it is still a good idea to get it planted in the spring so that you are not struggling to keep it well watered later on in the heat. Use a liquid feed weekly throughout the spring and summer and top-dress with organic matter in the spring (see page 44). After about five years, you will need to repot the tree to stop the plant becoming root-bound (see page 56).

COMMON PROBLEMS

Apricots should be pruned in summer (see page 54) to minimize the risk of silver leaf, a potentially fatal fungal disease that is most active in autumn and winter. Use netting to keep birds away from your precious fruit (see page 50).

LEMONS

I always think there is something very romantic about a lemon tree growing in a pot. Perhaps it is the way the scent of the blossom fills a room, or the knowledge that rich people in the past would build dedicated lemon houses to shelter their highly prized trees. Fortunately, even in a temperate climate such as the UK's, you do not have to go to quite such lengths, although the tree will need protection from frost. Lemons are hungry plants, so make sure you use a good, soil-based compost (potting soil), adding some grit or sharp sand to improve drainage. You can buy special composts for growing citrus, but I stick to my standard mix (see page 28).

In the kitchen, you will need only a couple of the fruits to make a zesty lemon tart, while one solitary fruit, preserved with some salt and aromatics (see page 218), will add a unique tangy flavour to a week's worth of dinners. And of course there is nothing like a gin and tonic flavoured with a lemon that you grew yourself. I promise you, it really does taste better.

FAVOURITE VARIETIES

'Meyer' is an excellent choice. Robust and widely available, it also flowers throughout the year, so is perfect for a container garden.

KEY DATES

Pot up new plants in late spring so that they can spend the whole summer and autumn getting established and toughen up before winter comes. Top-dress in spring (see page 44); this is also when you should repot established plants if they look to be losing vigour (see page 56). Lemons do not need much pruning; just cut back any damaged or unwanted growth in winter. They will need protection from the worst of the weather. In a temperate climate such as the UK's, and if you are growing in a sheltered spot, it may be enough to protect them in situ. But if you are in a country with colder winters, you really will have to find a place to keep them inside – a conservatory, porch or even a cool room will dramatically increase the chances of survival.

COMMON PROBLEMS

Overwatering is the most common cause of problems. Lemon trees like to dry out between waterings, so water them thoroughly once a week. I do mine every Tuesday. People tease me about my love of routine, but it does help me to remember. In winter, reduce the frequency of watering to once every ten days or even two weeks. You may also encounter scale insects – tiny parasitic bugs that look like bumps on the leaves. You can remove these by hand or with some damp cotton wool (cotton). A wipe with whisky seems to work wonders too, but don't use your finest single malt – the cheap stuff works just as well. As with all plants, fresh air is key to good health, so keep your lemon tree outside as much as possible, including on mild days during winter.

RHUBARB

Rhubarb is a perennial plant with a very large root system, but will grow well in a pot, provided it's at least 40 cm/16 inches in diameter. It is also very hungry, so make sure you use good compost (potting soil) and add plenty of organic matter (see page 28). Forced rhubarb is one of the gastronomic treats of the year, and is so easy to do with a pot. Just wait until the shoots start to emerge in early spring, then cover them to block out the light. A terracotta rhubarb forcer would look wonderful, but a plastic tub or trug will work equally well, provided there are no holes in it. Check under the cover every week or so to see whether the

shoots are starting to appear. The plants are unlikely to need water and won't need feeding at this stage. The resulting shoots are so pale and tender. Of course, you can just let the shoots develop normally, in which case they will be thicker and less pink, but still delicious to eat. Water well throughout the growing season. By mid-summer the stalks will be starting to get tougher and more acidic, and the plant will begin to run to seed. Don't fight it; there is nothing you can do anyway, and the flowers will look absolutely amazing in the pot.

FAVOURITE VARIETIES

I have to be honest and admit that the rhubarb at Great Dixter has been here since 1912 and its name is lost in the mists of time. That's rather a shame, since it is clearly a good one. 'Champagne' is an excellent variety that is easy to grow. It responds well to forcing and has particularly long slender stems, making it well suited to container growing. It also has a long season – some rhubarb is quick to develop an acidic flavour, but this variety stays sweet for months. If you are looking specifically for rhubarb to force, try 'Timperley Early', which, as the name suggests, is especially bred for early cropping.

KEY DATES

Plant rhubarb in the spring. In late autumn, clean up the dying stalks and leaves, and cover the crowns with a good layer of organic matter. While this will help to protect the plant through the winter, it will also add richness to the soil. If you are planning to force it, do so as soon as the shoots start to stir in early spring.

COMMON PROBLEMS

If rhubarb gets too wet in the winter, the crown can rot, which is fatal. There is nothing to do but tip it out and start again. In summer, you are likely to have the opposite problem. Rhubarb has big leaves, so will lose lots of water and, if it dries out, will run to seed very quickly. Water regularly and deeply at least twice a week to make sure this does not happen. When forcing rhubarb, watch for slugs under the cover. I use a few organically approved slug pellets to keep them at bay.

Growing Guide

HERBS

BASIL

Basil is ideally suited to being grown in a pot. To thrive, it needs as much heat and sun as you can give it, so move the pot around to keep it in the perfect spot as the summer progresses and the sun gets higher. Heat will concentrate the oils in the plant, intensifying the flavour and also scenting the air around it with the smell of a Mediterranean summer. Water it every couple of days. Basil is best eaten raw, torn up and sprinkled over tomatoes, grilled (broiled) vegetables or pasta, with nothing more than a little good olive oil. A word of warning, though: make sure you buy your pot of basil from a garden centre or nursery, not the supermarket. Those pots might look healthy, but the plants in there are overgrown and congested, and they will not survive being planted out.

FAVOURITE VARIETIES
'Sweet Genovese' is a great variety for the kitchen, with intense flavour and aroma. It also seems to do very well in a pot.

KEY DATES
There is no point sowing basil too early. It needs warmth and reasonably dry weather to really get going, so wait until mid-spring. If you prefer to buy seedlings, note the warning above about those supermarket pots.

COMMON PROBLEMS
Basil will struggle in a cool, damp summer. I have known seasons when I have had to give up on it altogether. If it's really flagging, try bringing it inside and putting it on the windowsill. The extra heat might just give it a boost and get it moving again. If that does the trick, put it back outside. Damp conditions can also cause mildew. Once your plants have it – look out for sickly yellow leaves, possibly with black spots – there is no choice but to pull them up and bin them (don't put them in your compost bin, if you have one, as the spores can spread). The best way to prevent mildew is to allow space between plants for air to circulate, and water from the base to avoid wetting the leaves.

CHIVES

This easy-going perennial is so useful in the kitchen, and it looks wonderful when in flower. The subtle onion flavour will enhance everything from a potato salad to a tomato sauce, and the flowers are delicious in a salad. The onion smell deters carrot fly, so it is an excellent idea to plant chives around the edge of the pot if you are growing carrots (see page 67). Chives can be grown from seed, or bought as a small plant from the garden centre, and are very easy to maintain. If they start to look a little sad later in the season, just cut them back and you will get fresh growth. Don't do them all at once, though, or you will be chive-less. Chives will die back in the winter, so you might want to add some other plants to the pot to keep it looking cheerful. Violas would be perfect. Just make sure they are not interfering with the young shoots when the chives start to grow again in the spring.

FAVOURITE VARIETIES
While there is only one species of chives – *Allium schoenoprasum* – the flowers come in a huge range of colours. I like the purple as dark as possible, but of course you won't know this until the plant flowers. One way around this is to keep an eye open for any good-looking chives in your friends' gardens and ask if you can dig some up there and then, or later in the year if they don't want any unsightly gaps. Remember, chives will need a lot of water to get them established if you're doing this in the summer.

KEY DATES
Sow seed or plant out in the spring. If you have an established plant, this is also a good time to up-end the pot and thin out the bulbs to stop it getting too congested.

COMMON PROBLEMS

Chives are pretty trouble-free. Keep them in tip-top condition with daily watering and regular picking to encourage good, fresh growth.

PARSLEY

Parsley could well be my number one annual herb (although, to be honest, there are a number of contenders for the top spot, as you will see). It's incredibly versatile in the kitchen, and very tough, remaining productive right through the year at Great Dixter, which is not the warmest spot in the world. In winter, it is a precious source of both fresh green flavour and vitamin C, and I love to eat it raw, either straight from the plant or as part of a salad. It's also brilliant in sauces and for adding both flavour and colour to tarts and even mashed potatoes. Parsley seeds also make a wonderfully flavoursome addition to a salad. If you can stop yourself eating them all, you can save some and use them for next year's crop (see page 30). Parsley will need frequent watering if it is to stay tender and not run to seed. Try to do it every day, especially if the weather is warm. Young plants may benefit from a cover on cold nights, just until they get going (see page 50).

FAVOURITE VARIETIES

Petroselinum crispum, more commonly known as 'French' or 'flat-leaf' parsley, is the one favoured by most cooks for its rich flavour. I had always dismissed curly parsley as flavourless stuff, only good for making sad little garnishes, until I tasted 'Moss Curled 2'. This brilliant herb flourishes right the way through winter, adding valuable flavour and colour to salads at a time when there are few fresh leaves around.

KEY DATES

Sow seed in early spring, or buy plug plants as soon as you see them for sale.

COMMON PROBLEMS

Parsley seeds can be slow to germinate in colder temperatures, so start them off on a windowsill inside, if possible. If you must direct sow outside, cover the pot with fleece (see page 231) to help the seeds get started.

MINT

Mint is an invasive perennial plant, with a great mat of roots. This makes it ideal for growing in pots, where it can be kept in check. Choose a big pot, 30 cm/12 inches across, as this is a vigorous plant. It is not worth growing mint from seed because it would take a long time to grow a decent-size plant. Plug plants are widely available and cheap, and you only need one. Just buy a pot from a garden centre or nursery – not the supermarket – when you see one for sale in the spring. You should only need to buy it once as mint is incredibly easy to propagate. Just cut short lengths of root – say, 5 cm/2 inches or so – lay them in a tray of compost (potting soil), cover thinly, keep moist and wait for the new growth to appear.

Mine came from my friend Laura Gatacre, and I am convinced it is less prone to mildew than plants I have had in the past.

KEY DATES
Cut mint back to the ground in spring, then mulch (see page 43), feed and water well. You will also need to do this again in the summer. Ideally, do it just before a holiday (having arranged for someone to do the watering while you're away, of course) so that you come back to wonderful fresh growth.

COMMON PROBLEMS
The main challenge is to keep the growth fresh, as mint is prone to powdery mildew (see page 232) in the summer. The only real remedy is to cut it down to the ground and let it start again. If you are concerned about being without mint for a while, grow two pots and stagger the cutting.

LOVAGE

Lovage is a useful perennial herb, particularly in the early spring before the celery and celeriac (celery root) are ready. It's invaluable for adding that distinctive flavour to stocks (broths) and soups. It looks very handsome too, with its pinkish-tinged stems and fresh green leaves, rather like a more dramatic version of parsley. Do be careful, though – the flavour is very intense, but it will mellow somewhat with cooking. When using lovage in a salad, I often rub a couple of leaves around the salad bowl and discard them before adding the other ingredients. That will be enough to release the oils and impart the flavour. Lovage has a large taproot, shaped rather like a carrot, so will need a sturdy, deep pot around 30 cm/12 inches in diameter. Direct sow the seeds to avoid later disturbance, and don't be tempted to sow too many. Even one plant will give you more leaves than you can possibly hope to use. Lovage doesn't need much water: a soaking every four days or so will be enough.

Every spring, I give the plant a good tidying, first removing any growth, then tipping it out of the pot and thinning the roots before repotting, top-dressing with organic matter (see page 44) and giving it a good feed with blood, fish and bone meal (see page 231). It then gets another haircut in mid-summer, the only remedy for the mildew that will inevitably afflict it at some point. Regular picking will help to avoid this by encouraging the plant to put on more growth. Water daily. Mint is a vigorous plant and will quickly run to seed if it gets stressed.

Young leaves taste the best and are perfect for mojitos (see page 224). Mint is also a brilliant partner for anything involving peas or salad potatoes (see pages 164 and 183).

FAVOURITE VARIETIES
Mentha spicata, or common garden mint, is the one I grow. If you have a friend with a healthy plant, ask if you can have a bit of it in the spring.

FAVOURITE VARIETIES
There is really only one species, *Levisticum officinale.* Given a big enough pot, it will grow

up to 1.8 m/6 feet tall. In summer, it has a flat-headed flower like that of yellow cow parsley.

KEY DATES
Ideally, sow in autumn so that you have good growth by early spring. This is a Mediterranean plant, so new shoots will start to appear in the winter. Protect them by covering with fleece (see page 231) if the weather is very cold.

COMMON PROBLEMS
Lovage is prone to leaf miners – moth larvae that tunnel their way through the leaves, making them warty and bumpy. I just remove the affected leaves.

CORIANDER (CILANTRO)

The great thing about coriander is that you can use the whole plant. I add the leaves and flowers to salads; I use the seeds in Christopher Lloyd's recipe for salad dressing (just grind some seeds with salt and pepper, before adding mustard,

vinegar and oil to taste); and even the root can be used as a flavouring for curries or soups – try it with carrot. I sow coriander direct, protecting the pot with fleece (see page 231) until germination is under way. As you use the plants or they run to seed, just pop more seeds into the gaps and water them in to ensure a succession. Anything sown in spring or summer will eventually run to seed, no matter how diligent you are about picking. Don't fight it! Just enjoy the flowers and seeds instead. I find that seed you have saved yourself (see page 30) is stronger tasting and more aromatic than anything you can buy. A final late sowing of this herb at the end of the summer should keep you in leaves through the winter if you are gardening in a temperate climate.

FAVOURITE VARIETIES
For leaves, I choose bolt-resistant varieties, such as 'Cruiser'. For good-size, flavoursome seeds I like 'Santo Monogerm', which I get from the wonderful Johnny's Selected Seeds.

KEY DATES
Try to get your first sowing done in early spring. After that, every month or so throughout the growing season, pop a few seeds into any gaps. If you keep sowing until late summer/early autumn, you can keep a crop going into the winter.

COMMON PROBLEMS
Germination can be slow if the spring is cold and wet. Cover with fleece to speed things up. In summer, your main challenge will be stopping the plants running to seed before you want them to. Daily watering and regular picking will help to delay the inevitable.

DILL

With its feathery leaves and bright yellow, umbel-shaped flowers floating above the other crops, dill is great for adding visual interest to the container herb garden. Try putting a pot or two of this perennial herb among your lettuces, both for the visual effect and to cast a little dappled shade. I grow dill both for its leaves – wonderful as a stuffing or in a sauce for salmon or trout,

with new potatoes, or just raw in a salad – and its seeds. These are delicious in a salad, or stirred into good olive oil and eaten with some fresh bread. Dill does best from direct sowing, as it does not like its roots disturbed. It will thrive in a pot, provided you water every couple of days and do not let it dry out. Otherwise, you will find you have a good crop of seeds rather earlier than you might have liked.

FAVOURITE VARIETIES
I grow *Anethum graveolens* for its beautiful leaves, which look rather like those of fennel. For a good crop of decent-size seeds, I like 'Mammoth', which also does very well as a cut flower.

KEY DATES
Direct sow in early spring. Cover the soil surface with fleece (see page 231) to get the seeds going. You can start picking once the plants are about 15 cm/6 inches tall and have a decent amount of leaves on them. Every month, pop a few more seeds into the spaces in the pot to ensure a continuous supply.

COMMON PROBLEMS
Dill is prone to damping-off (see page 231), or going mouldy. The key to avoiding this is not to stint on watering, but rather to add some sharp sand to the soil before planting (see page 29) and make sure the pot is in a sunny spot. Also give each plant enough space for air to circulate around it; 5–10 cm/2–4 inches is perfect.

TARRAGON

Tarragon may not be the best-looking herb in the container garden, but for me it is one of the most useful. The only problem I have with it is growing enough to keep pace with demand. I always have several pots on the go at any one time, as I can get through an entire plant in a day when I am cooking tarragon chicken for a crowd. I also like to use it raw in a salad, particularly alongside fish, and it is wonderful with trout baked in newspaper (see page 146). Tarragon is perennial, but it will need some protection to get it through the winter.

I am lucky to have access to a neighbour's greenhouse, so I can keep a supply going all year round.

FAVOURITE VARIETIES
There is only one species to grow, *Artemisia dracunculus* or French tarragon. Avoid Russian tarragon (*Artemisia dracunculoides*) at all costs. It may grow faster, but it is tough and lacking in flavour.

KEY DATES
French tarragon does not set viable seed, so if you are starting from scratch, buy a plant from a garden centre (one will be enough to see a normal household through the summer) and pot it up in early spring. Mine is in a pot 20 cm/ 8 inches across. If you already have a plant, cut it back and repot in fresh compost (potting soil). It will need shelter in the winter, so if you don't have anywhere else to put it, bring it inside. It will grow softer, but at least it will survive. Keep well watered in the heat of summer to ensure that you always have good, fresh growth. A decent watering twice a week should be enough. If the

plant starts to get woody and tired-looking late in the season, cut it back again. In a mild autumn, it will continue to produce fresh leaves. The plants will need replacing every few years, when they start to look less vigorous.

COMMON PROBLEMS
Tarragon is prone to rust (see page 232), an airborne fungal disease. Regular picking will help to reduce this problem, as new growth is less susceptible than older leaves. If your plant does succumb and you start to see rust-coloured pustules appear, cut it to the ground, top-dress (see page 44), water well and start again.

BAY LAUREL

Bay laurel is a great choice for adding structure to your container garden and, as an evergreen, will keep its good looks all year round. Of course, being handsome is not enough by itself; fortunately, bay is extremely useful in the kitchen too. It adds flavour and fragrance to soups, stews and slow-cooked meats, but is also great in desserts – try adding some to stewed apple, or even substituting it for fig leaves to make a wonderfully aromatic ice-cream (see page 194). A bay tree is very easy to look after, provided you give it a good sunny spot and feed it regularly. Prune every spring, both to keep it at the size you want it and to reduce any congestion. Like any large plant grown in a container, bay laurel will benefit from repotting every few years to keep it vigorous and encourage fresh new growth (see page 56).

FAVOURITE VARIETIES
Laurus nobilis is the variety used in cooking. Try throwing a branch on the fire too – the oils in the leaves will release their fragrance and scent the whole room.

KEY DATES
Buy young plants in spring and plant them out once any danger of frost is past. They will need weekly watering and regular doses of liquid feed during the summer, when they are putting on growth. Protect young plants in winter: a layer of

fleece (see page 231) will do if you are gardening in a temperate climate; in colder conditions you will need to move your plant inside, to a cool, well-ventilated spot. If you intend to prune your bay into exciting shapes, do this in late spring, again waiting until the frosts are over.

COMMON PROBLEMS
Bay is popular with scale insects, so look out for the small brown bugs on leaves and stems. In hot weather it is also prone to sooty mould. In both cases, the best remedy is a very simple one – a good wash with soapy water.

ROSEMARY

Mediterranean herbs do particularly well in containers. These forgiving perennial plants actually seem to thrive on harsh treatment, requiring little more than a decent dose of sunshine to concentrate their oils and maximize flavour. Indeed, the harder they are grown, the more flavour they seem to have.

Rosemary is best grown from plants rather than seed and needs a good, long growing season so that it can toughen up a bit before winter. Add some sand or grit to the pot when planting up to make them feel at home. Throw some fleece (see page 231) over it on particularly chilly nights or, if you are gardening in a cold climate, bring it inside for the winter. Put it somewhere cool, with good ventilation.

When choosing what variety of rosemary to grow, you will need to consider the colour – the flowers are most commonly blue, but also come in white and pink – and the habit. Prostrate rosemary will look beautiful grown around the edges of a pot, while a more upright variety will make a wonderful focal point for the garden.

In the kitchen, rosemary with roast lamb has become a cliché for a good reason – it is absolutely wonderful, provided you don't overdo it. I also love it on roast potatoes, with a good sprinkling of sea salt, and added to a jug (pitcher) of iced water on a hot summer's day.

FAVOURITE VARIETIES

There are many named cultivars of *Rosmarinus officinalis*, and most make for good eating. Choose the colour and habit that appeals, and also check the label – some will be more strongly flavoured than others, and therefore more useful in the kitchen. I particularly like the trailing habit of those in the 'Prostratus' group. Try growing some of these around the edge of a pot of dill (see page 98) – a stunning combination.

KEY DATES

Plant out new plants, and prune established ones, in late spring, after the frosts. Pruning is important to encourage fresh growth, as rosemary can become very woody over time. You can also give it a haircut in summer, once the flowers are over.

COMMON PROBLEMS

As the name suggests, rosemary beetles are fond of rosemary, as well as other aromatic plants such as thyme (see below), sage and lavender. This is more likely to be a problem in warmer climates. If you spot the small, metallic green bugs, pull them off and squash them. Not very pleasant, but effective. Avoid overwatering these sun-lovers, or they will lose their flavour and rot. Once a week in summer is plenty.

THYME

Like rosemary (see above), thyme will do very well in a pot. Think shallow dishes and troughs, where the water can easily drain away, and make sure you add some sand or horticultural grit to the soil (see page 29). Water and feed it well after pruning (see Key dates), and fresh new growth will soon appear. The rest of the time water sparingly – once a week is fine.

This perennial herb is a wonderful ground-cover plant, so put it where you are going to brush against it, releasing the scent. Alternatively, plant it around the base of a fruit tree: this will increase your growing space, suppress weeds and help to retain moisture in the soil. You can grow thyme from seed – something that I will be experimenting with

for the leaf and flower colour that appeals to you. I also like to grow lemon thyme, but it has a completely different flavour from common thyme, so should not be regarded as a substitute.

KEY DATES
As with rosemary, young plants need a chance to establish themselves before the cold comes, so get them planted up as soon as the frosts have passed. Prune thyme in summer, after flowering, to stop it getting too woody.

COMMON PROBLEMS
Thyme hates to get its feet wet, and will rot off in the winter if it sits in water. To avoid this, use a good, free-draining compost (potting soil) with some added grit or sand and put the plant in a shallow pot.

LEMON VERBENA

Smells and flavours can be incredibly evocative, and the fragrance of lemon verbena tea instantly transports me to the glasshouse at the Jerusalem Botanical Gardens in the height of summer. Lemon verbena is pretty hardy, and very easy to grow from a plug plant in a pot. As with mint (see page 96), this perennial plant would take forever to grow to a decent size from seed, and since you only need one it makes sense to just buy it. If you are starting from scratch, look out for a strong young plant and pot up in spring. The longer it spends outside, the more chance it will stand of making it through the winter. You can help it along by bringing it close to the house, and being ready with the fleece (see page 231) if the temperature drops. You can use the young leaves to make tea in the summer – try it iced on particularly hot days – and dry some to use over the winter, as it will keep its fragrance very well. It can also be used to flavour ice-creams, custards and cakes, and even to scent a bath. In the UK climate, lemon verbena will usually overwinter outside, provided it is in a sheltered spot. Throw some fleece over it if there is a cold snap. When your plant starts to look tired, take some cuttings from it and start again.

soon – but if you want to get your hands on some fairly quickly, buy thyme plants from a garden centre.

Thyme offers a wide variety of flower and foliage colours. In the past I have put plants of different leaf colours – say silver, deep green and golden – together in a single large pot to create a mosaic effect, which was most effective. To add to its virtues, thyme is one of the best plants for attracting bees to your container garden. Of course, it is also extremely useful in the kitchen. I use it in soups and stews, and I love to use it in Creamed Chicken (see page 140). But it is perhaps best added to dishes that are being roasted, grilled (broiled) or even barbecued because the intense heat will bring out the oils and maximize the flavour.

FAVOURITE VARIETIES
Make sure you are buying culinary rather than ornamental thyme. *Thymus vulgaris* or common thyme is the default variety. Beyond this, there is a huge range of cultivars to choose from. Go

Growing Guide

FAVOURITE VARIETIES

There is only one, *Aloysia triphylla*, which is native to parts of South America. It forms an attractive shrub, growing to about 45 cm/ 18 inches tall in a container, with elegantly pointed, very fragrant leaves.

KEY DATES

Once you have an established plant, spring is the time to prune out any winter damage and to take cuttings if you would like to increase your stock. They should be taken from the previous year's growth – not too fresh and soft, but not too woody either. Use a sharp pair of secateurs (pruning shears) so that you get a clean cut and don't damage the stem tissue. Trim cuttings to 5 cm/2 inches long, with about three sets of leaves. Cut the leaves in half widthwise. This will help to minimize water loss while the plant gets established, while keeping enough of the leaf for the plant to photosynthesize. Pop the cuttings into a small pot of free-draining compost (potting soil), put a plastic bag over the top and place on the windowsill. Remember to lift the cover off regularly so that they get some air, which will stop them rotting.

COMMON PROBLEMS

Generally, lemon verbena is pretty trouble-free. If the winter is particularly cold and you decide to bring the plant in, it may suffer from whitefly (see page 233) or red spider mite. The best cure is simply to put it outside again. Just as with people, a good dose of fresh air will cure most ills. Avoid overwatering or you will dilute the herb's flavour and risk rotting the plant.

OREGANO

Another great choice for a shallow pot, oregano is an intensely flavoured perennial herb that goes beautifully with Mediterranean foods. Think grilled (broiled) lamb, roasted vegetables and anything involving tomato. My recommendation is to buy oregano plants rather than trying to grow them from seed because it would take a long time to grow a decent-size plant from seed. You will need only one or two, so it is well worth

saving yourself the time. Oregano needs a free-draining soil, so add some sand or grit when potting up (see page 29). Give the plants as much sun as possible to concentrate the oils and maximize the flavour.

FAVOURITE VARIETIES

Look no further than the standard issue *Origanum vulgare*. It is widely available and has an excellent flavour. I also like its small purple flowers, as do the bees.

KEY DATES

Buy and pot up new plants in spring. Established plants should survive the winter, although they might look a little sad. In this case, cut them back and give them a good top-dressing with, for example, worm compost (see pages 29 and 44) to kick-start their growth for the new season.

COMMON PROBLEMS

Like all the Mediterranean herbs, oregano is prone to rotting if overwet, so make sure the soil is free-draining by adding some sand or grit to the potting mix (see above) and keep it in the sunniest spot you can find.

NASTURTIUMS

The first thing to say about nasturtiums is: keep them under control. Pick the flowers regularly to keep them blooming and stop them running to seed quite so quickly. Once the seeds start to form, you can harvest and dry them (see page 30). They, just like the flowers and leaves, make an excellent peppery addition to a salad, and you can even pickle the seeds if you wish – they taste rather like capers. Inevitably, some of the seeds will spread themselves around and germinate. If they're growing in the wrong place or you have more than you need, pull the whole plant out. It is tempting to leave them to do their thing because they look so beautiful, but you do have to remind them who's boss.

Nasturtiums will do best grown in full sun, but beyond that these annual plants are gloriously unfussy and will thrive in poor soil and be grateful for whatever water you give them, so are perfect for growing in containers. Just dot a few seeds in among your pots as the weather warms up, poking them in close to the edge so they will trail over the side. Don't overdo it – remember, these are vigorous plants. I would not plant more than one in a pot, unless the pot was very large, and then I would leave at least 20 cm/8 inches between the seeds.

FAVOURITE VARIETIES
I like 'Variegatus' for its trailing habit, bright green leaves and vibrant red and orange flowers.

KEY DATES
Direct sow from mid- to late spring. You can start nasturtiums off in a pot on the windowsill if you wish, but they do so well outside that there is really no need.

COMMON PROBLEMS
Nasturtiums are prone to pests such as flea beetles, caterpillars, aphids, slugs and whitefly. Use this to your advantage to keep these pests off your other crops. If the plants are really badly affected, just pull them out and tuck a couple of fresh seeds in their place. See page 233 for more on how to deal with common pests.

VIOLAS

Violas could well be my number one edible flower to grow, but I must confess that I cannot bring myself to eat them. Their little faces are just too sweet. But that is not to say these annual plants aren't performing a useful role in the container garden, covering the empty spaces at the base of trees, shrubs and perennial vegetables, such as globe artichokes (see page 78), which die back in the winter. They provide a great deal of interest in the cold months when little else is happening. Of course, if you are made of tougher stuff than me, you can add them to salads, desserts or fruit. Despite their delicate appearance, violas are fairly robust and

will get by on relatively little water. They will also happily self-sow, although you can point them in the right direction by sprinkling a few seeds into any cracks in the paving.

FAVOURITE VARIETIES
'Helen Mount' is a long-standing favourite, with the classic viola combination of purple, yellow and mauve. I also grow 'Bunny Ears', which is the most beautiful reddish-purple and has pointed upper petals, just like a pair of rabbit's ears.

KEY DATES
I sow seed in early spring, then again in late summer, to ensure I have violas through the winter. Generally, I will sow into a 10-cm/4-inch pot and prick out the seedlings into plug trays once they have two true leaves (see pages 32 and 35). In a particularly warm spring, you can sow direct. I do find, though, that the strongest and most successful plants are the ones that sow themselves, so once you have violas established in your garden, you can pretty much leave them to it.

COMMON PROBLEMS
Violas like space and sunshine. If they are too crowded, they do not do well, so plant them around the edge of the pot, leaving a handspan between each plant. If you have self-sowers, you will need to thin them out to give each plant space to develop.

SCENTED-LEAF PELARGONIUMS

My collection of scented pelargoniums is rather like an alternative photo album. They are grown from cuttings I have taken all over the world, and they are a great reminder of those places and the people I love.

Scented pelargoniums bring so much to the container garden. The foliage effect is wonderful, and of course there is the scent, so evocative and so delicious as a flavouring for sorbets and syrups. Buy young plants from a garden centre or nursery in spring and pot them on immediately into a slightly larger pot using

good, free-draining compost (potting soil). They will thank you for adding a bit of grit or sharp sand to the mix (see page 29). If the nights are still cold, bring your plants in and keep them on a windowsill overnight until the danger of frost has passed. This will make them soft, so do put them outside for a dose of fresh air whenever the weather permits. If you prefer, or if the plants are too big to bring inside, wrap them in fleece instead (see page 231).

In the UK scented pelargoniums can be treated as tender perennials, which means they will come back every year, but will need protection through the winter. I have mine outside for eight months of the year – the tougher you treat them, the stronger they will be and the more likely they are to get through the winter. In a colder climate, they will need to be kept under cover throughout the winter. The same principle applies to water and fertilizer – too much of either and they will grow leggy, soft and weak. Their dense foliage also tends to trap moisture, and if overwatered, they can rot or go mouldy. Remember, these are plants that thrive in hot dry climates.

FAVOURITE VARIETIES
For me the number one has to be 'Attar of Roses', with its definitive rose geranium scent and delicate pink flowers.

KEY DATES
In spring, cut the plants back by about two-thirds and fork a bit of blood, fish and bone meal (see page 231) into the soil.

COMMON PROBLEMS
Whitefly (see page 233) can be a problem, particularly when the plants are inside for the winter. Putting them outside as often as you can will help; on a nice sunny winter's day, they won't come to any harm. You might also encounter the odd caterpillar. The best way to deal with these is to pick them off and squash them.

FRENCH MARIGOLDS

Marigolds are a very nostalgic flower for me. My grandmother loved to grow them, although I think it was more for their vibrant colour than their edible petals. I grow these annual plants for both these reasons, and also because they are such a useful companion plant. Their pungent smell helps to keep whitefly and aphids (see page 233) away from other crops. I tend to grow a few together in a single pot, and use it as a sort of portable pest control device, moving it to wherever the need is greatest at the time.

    The flowers have a mild citrus flavour and are very good in salads, with fish and to decorate desserts. If you pick the flower heads regularly, your marigolds should keep blooming throughout the summer.

FAVOURITE VARIETIES
My great friend Dr Kyle usually pops a packet of 'Durango Outback Mix' in with my seed parcel, and I am very glad that she does. This variety is a low-growing marigold, but it branches well and ultimately covers a good area. It also has the loveliest mix of sunset colours. 'Paprika' is another good choice for pots, as it tends to form a neat mound. It has deep red flowers with a yellow centre, and finely cut, scented foliage.

Position your marigolds somewhere you will brush against them to release their scent.

KEY DATES
Sow seed in early spring, and cover the pot with fleece (see page 231) to encourage germination.

COMMON PROBLEMS
The seeds have a tendency to clump together, making it difficult to sow them thinly. If your seedlings are overcrowded, thin them out and replant the excess ones in another pot. Each plant should have about 15 cm/6 inches of space around it to allow air to circulate and avoid rotting. These are big-leaved plants, so will need plenty of water, but they are used to tough environments, so provided you plant them into a good soil-based compost (potting soil), they are unlikely to need feeding. Tall varieties might need staking, in which case use bamboo canes and garden twine, tying them securely enough to give support but not so tightly that they snap in the first breeze. See page 46 for more about supporting plants.

BREAKFAST

BIRCHER MUESLI

BREAKFAST MUFFINS

BREAKFAST SALAD

BRAISED CHICORY WITH EGGS

POTATO AND PARSNIP FARLS

CANNELLINI BEANS ON TOAST WITH
CRISPY KALE

BIRCHER MUESLI

Serves 4 generously, with leftovers

Siew Lee, a colleague at Great Dixter, is a great gardener and also a very talented cook. Siew has lived all over the world and picked up some great recipes along the way, including this one – a souvenir of her time in Switzerland. Oats make a fantastic breakfast, and will keep the wolf at bay until lunchtime. This recipe is great for using small amounts of seasonal fruit, whether you're picking it fresh or have a few small bags stashed away in the freezer. You'll need to soak the oats for at least 1½ hours to soften properly, so be sure to start this recipe the night before. Adding cream instead of yogurt makes this into a rather luxurious dish, although arguably a slightly less healthy one. If I am making it with cream I particularly like to use tart fruit such as fresh currants or gooseberries, to cut through the richness.

Put the oats, milk or juice and nuts, if using, in a large bowl and mix well. Cover and leave in the refrigerator overnight, or for at least 1½ hours.

When you are ready to eat, add the yogurt or cream and fruit and stir through. Sweeten to taste: I like to use honey, but demerara (turbinado) sugar sprinkled on top will give a good crunch.

If you're planning to snack on the muesli throughout the day, don't add all the soft fruit at once as it will go mushy – you can add it just before you plan to eat. Without the soft fruit, the muesli mix will keep perfectly well in the refrigerator for a couple of days.

PREPARATION: 20 minutes,
   plus overnight soaking

100 g/3½ oz (1¼ cups) fine porridge
   (steel-cut) oats
50 g/2 oz (½ cup) rolled oats
600 ml/1 pint (2½ cups) milk or fruit
   juice (apple or orange)
100 g/3½ oz (⅔ cup) almonds
   or hazelnuts, coarsely chopped
   (optional)
450 g/1 lb (1¾ cups) plain yogurt
   (use dairy-free if you prefer)
   or double (heavy) cream, or
   a mixture of cream and yogurt
2 apples, coarsely grated
2 bananas, sliced
1 orange, peeled and cut into chunks
200 g/7 oz soft fruit, such as
   apricots, raspberries, currants,
   gooseberries, blueberries, stewed
   apples or plums (either fresh
   or from the freezer), chopped
   if necessary into bite-size pieces
   (1⅓ cups prepared)
handful dried fruit, chopped if
   necessary into bite-size pieces
honey or demerara (turbinado)
   sugar, to taste

BREAKFAST MUFFINS

Makes 12 large muffins or 16 regular muffins

I remember this recipe from my childhood. My father, who was very ahead of his time with regard to healthy eating, was always making things like this. A lot of his friends were hippies, and I think he was probably the number-one customer at our local health-food store. Nevertheless, he was not one to don a hair shirt for the sake of it – flavour always came first in his cooking. Whenever he made these muffins, our friends next door would come running over for breakfast, drawn in by the delicious smell of baking. The fruit can be varied to suit the season. Try adding raspberries, blackcurrants or grated apple instead of the fresh figs. You can change the flavour of the jam you use too, to suit.

Preheat the oven to 180°C/350°F/Gas Mark 4. Line a baking sheet with baking (parchment) paper. Butter and flour the holes of a jumbo muffin pan, or 16 holes of 2 non-stick 12-hole muffin pans.

Spread out the wheat bran on the prepared baking sheet and bake for 5 minutes, or until lightly toasted. Remove from the oven, turn the bran over once or twice and return to the oven for another 5 minutes.

In a large bowl, mix together the toasted wheat bran, yogurt, lemon zest, honey, fig jam and soft brown sugar. Add 250 ml/ 8 fl oz (1 cup) water, the oil, egg and egg white and mix until well combined.

Sift the flours, baking powder, bicarbonate of soda (baking soda), cinnamon, nutmeg and salt into a large bowl. Stir into the wet ingredients, add the pumpkin seeds and mix until just combined, being sure to not over-mix.

Spoon the batter into the prepared pan(s), filling each hole almost to the top. Top each one with 2 fig slices. Bake in the oven for 25 minutes, or until a skewer inserted into the middle of a muffin comes out clean.

Let cool in the pan(s) for 5 minutes before transferring to a wire rack to cool completely. Sprinkle a little demerara (turbinado) sugar over the muffins before serving.

PREPARATION: 30 minutes
COOKING: 35 minutes

butter, for greasing
120 g/4 oz (2 cups) wheat bran
120 g/4 oz (½ cup) plain yogurt
½ tablespoon grated lemon zest
1 tablespoon honey
3 tablespoons fig jam
120 g/4 oz (½ cup packed) soft light
   brown sugar
120 ml/4 fl oz (½ cup) sunflower oil
1 egg, plus 1 egg white
65 g/2½ oz (½ cup) plain (all-
   purpose) flour, plus extra for
   dusting
65 g/2½ oz (½ cup) wholemeal
   (whole-wheat) flour
1 teaspoon baking powder
1 teaspoon bicarbonate of soda
   (baking soda)
½ teaspoon ground cinnamon
½ teaspoon ground nutmeg
pinch of salt
50 g/2 oz (⅓ cup) pumpkin seeds,
   coarsely chopped
6 figs, de-stemmed and each cut
   across into 6 slices
demerara (turbinado) sugar,
   for sprinkling

BREAKFAST SALAD

Serves 2

Sometimes you meet people who live their lives in such a great way that you cannot help but be impressed. I felt like this when I went to Detroit and met Greg and Olivia, the owners of Brother Nature Farm. They specialize in leafy salad (greens) crops, and have even developed their own cut-and-come-again seed variety. So I suppose it's not surprising that they even eat salad for breakfast. They use a spicy mix that includes sorrel, mizuna and rocket (arugula), but you can use whatever you have to hand, including rocket, parsley, tarragon, coriander (cilantro) and even dandelion leaves if you're a bit behind on the weeding. If you're using a lot of these strong-flavoured leaves a handful of lettuce leaves will help calm the mix down and give you the right balance of punchy flavour and cool refreshment. I love this at the start of a day spent working outside, but it also makes a great quick and healthy lunch.

PREPARATION: 20 minutes
COOKING: 5 minutes

120 ml/4 fl oz (½ cup) good-quality oil – Greg and Olivia use rapeseed (canola) oil, but you can use olive oil if you prefer
2 tablespoons (apple) cider vinegar
4 handfuls mixed salad leaves (greens)
1 apple, cored and cut into slivers
small handful radishes, thinly sliced
2 really fresh eggs
8 or so nasturtium flowers (optional) (you can also add nasturtium leaves to the salad leaves/greens for an extra peppery kick)
salt and pepper

Make a dressing by mixing together the oil and vinegar and then seasoning with salt and pepper.

Wash and dry the salad leaves (greens) thoroughly – I use a salad spinner. Put the salad leaves, apple and radishes in a large bowl and then add the dressing, a little at a time, and toss well. You want everything to be coated in the dressing, but not drowned.

Fill a pan with no less than 5 cm/2 inches of water and crack the eggs into ramekins. Bring the water to a gentle simmer, then gently slide the eggs into the water and cook for 3–5 minutes until the whites are set but the yolks still runny. Remove the eggs with a slotted spoon and drain briefly on paper towels.

Top the salad with the nasturtium flowers, if using, and poached eggs, season with pepper and serve.

BRAISED CHICORY WITH EGGS

Serves 2

I like to eat this on a weekend when my friends Flora and Jonny are staying with me. They are great wild swimmers, so when they are here we will often get up and run down to the River Rother for a swim first thing in the morning. This dish is a wonderful reward for our exertions. Braising chicory adds a mellow sweetness to temper this vegetable's distinctive bitter edge.

Fill a pan with no less than 5 cm/2 inches of water and crack the eggs into ramekins. Bring the water to a gentle simmer, then gently slide the eggs into the water and cook for 3 minutes, or until the whites are set but the yolks still runny. Using a slotted spoon, transfer the eggs to a plate and set aside. Leave the water over low heat.

Slice the chicory (Belgian endive) heads in half lengthwise, then slice each half across into chunky strips about as thick as your finger. Check for dirt and rinse if necessary.

In a pan, warm the oil, add the leek and cook over medium–low heat until soft – about 5 minutes. Increase the heat, add the garlic and chicory and cook for about 5 minutes, until the chicory has slightly softened. Add the stock (broth), reduce the heat and simmer gently, covered, for 5 minutes, or until the chicory is soft. Season to taste with salt and pepper. (The same method applies if you are using greens, although you will not need to caramelize them. Just stir with the garlic and oil to coat, before adding the stock. Kale will take a little longer to soften.)

Toast the bread and then, while the bread is still warm, rub one side with a cut piece of raw garlic. Place each slice of bread into a warmed shallow bowl and spoon over the chicory and braising liquid so that the bread soaks it up.

Slide the poached eggs back into the simmering water and cook for 30 seconds. Remove the eggs with a slotted spoon and drain briefly on paper towels. Top the chicory with the eggs, season with salt and pepper and sprinkle with chopped chives and pul biber or chilli flakes, if using, and serve.

PREPARATION: 30 minutes
COOKING: 20 minutes

2–4 really fresh eggs
2 large heads of chicory (Belgian endive) – you want about 1 head per person (or 250 g/9 oz/5 cups prepared greens per person, such as kale, Swiss chard or perpetual spinach)
5 tablespoons good-quality extra virgin olive oil
1 leek, trimmed and diced
2 cloves garlic, sliced, plus 1 extra peeled clove for rubbing on the bread
2 tablespoons chicken or vegetable stock (broth)
2 thick slices bread, such as sourdough
salt and pepper

TO GARNISH
finely chopped chives
pul biber or chilli flakes (optional)

POTATO AND PARSNIP FARLS

Serves 4–6

This recipe comes to me from my friend Jonny Bruce, who remembers eating these farls on childhood trips to Ireland. These farls are great for a weekend brunch – just add sausages, roasted tomatoes and a poached or fried egg to create your own container garden big breakfast. They are also perfect with a few shavings of strong Cheddar. If you don't want to make all the farls at once, the dough will keep in the refrigerator for a couple of days. Alternatively, you can reheat cooked farls in the toaster.

PREPARATION: 20 minutes
COOKING: 30 minutes

250 g/9 oz (about 2) floury (baking) potatoes (or about 200 g/7 oz/1 cup leftover mashed potatoes)
200 g/7 oz (about 2) parsnips (weight after you have trimmed and peeled them)
40 g/1½ oz (3 tablespoons) unsalted butter
2 tablespoons chopped dill
2 tablespoons chopped flat-leaf parsley
50 g/2 oz (⅓ cup plus 1 tablespoon) plain (all-purpose) flour, plus extra for dusting
salt and pepper

TO SERVE
roasted tomatoes
fried eggs
fried sausages

Scrub and coarsely chop the potatoes. (I never peel potatoes for mashing – life is too short.) Put the potatoes and parsnips into a large pan of salted water, bring to a boil and cook until tender – about 20 minutes. Drain the vegetables, leaving them in the colander until the steam has died down and they are properly dried. Tip them back into the empty pan and mash with the butter. Season generously with salt and pepper. Add the herbs, then sift in the flour and mix with a wooden spoon to form a rough dough.

Lightly flour a work counter. Take one-third of the dough and knead it lightly into a ball, then use the heel of your hand to press it into a 13-cm/5-inch disc that is just under 1 cm/½ inch thick. It's important to keep the work counter well floured as the mixture can be sticky.

Heat a non-stick frying pan or skillet over medium heat. Slide in the potato cake (you do not need to add any oil or butter) and cook for 2½–3 minutes until golden brown underneath, then flip over and cook for another 2½–3 minutes. The farl will start to puff up slightly when it's done. Cut the farl into 4 with a spatula (the word 'farl' comes from the Gaelic word for 'four', according to Jonny) and keep warm in a low oven. Repeat with the remaining dough.

Serve with roasted tomatoes, fried eggs and sausages (or leave out the sausages for a vegetarian version). You could also add other vegetables from your container garden, for example some wilted spinach, or bell peppers added in with the tomatoes when roasting.

Breakfast

CANNELLINI BEANS ON TOAST WITH CRISPY KALE

Serves 2

I love this dish. It's hearty but light, and the kale adds a real intensity of flavour – as well as a great contrast in texture – that cuts through the sweetness of the beans and tomatoes. It's a perfect way to refuel after an energetic start to the day, but it also makes a great lunch. The bread is important here; you need a good-quality, substantial loaf, so it can soak up the juices and flavours without disintegrating. In the winter, when the kale is still in peak condition, this recipe will work perfectly well with a couple of canned plum tomatoes too.

PREPARATION: 20 minutes
COOKING: 15 minutes

4 really fresh eggs
100 g/3½ oz prepared curly kale, washed, dried and coarsely chopped (1½ cups chopped)
5 tablespoons extra virgin olive oil
grated zest of 1 lemon
4 good-size tomatoes, or 8–10 cherry tomatoes, cored, if necessary, and coarsely chopped
1 clove garlic, crushed (minced)
1–2 thyme sprigs, leaves stripped from the stems
1 x 400-g/14-oz can cannellini beans, drained and rinsed
bread, for toasting – 1–2 slices each, depending on appetite and the heftiness of your bread
2 tablespoons pumpkin seeds
salt and pepper

Preheat the oven to 180°C/350°F/Gas Mark 4.

Fill a pan with no less than 5 cm/2 inches of water and crack the eggs into ramekins. Bring the water to a gentle simmer, then gently slide the eggs into the water and cook for 3 minutes, or until the whites are set but the yolks still runny. Using a slotted spoon, transfer the eggs to a plate and set aside. Leave the water over low heat.

Put the kale into a bowl, add 2 tablespoons of the oil, the lemon zest and ¼ teaspoon of salt and massage the ingredients into the leaves. Spread the leaves out over the bottom of a large roasting pan or baking sheet and bake for 10–12 minutes, turning once or twice during cooking, until crisp. Remove and set aside.

Meanwhile, warm the remaining oil in a pan. Add the tomatoes to the pan along with the garlic and thyme. Cook over medium heat for 8–10 minutes until the tomatoes have started to break down a little and some of their juices have been driven off – you don't want the mixture to be too watery. Add the beans to the pan and gently warm through, then season to taste with salt and pepper.

Toast your bread. Slide the eggs back into the simmering water and cook for 30 seconds. Remove the eggs with a slotted spoon and drain briefly on paper towels. Place the toast onto warmed plates, spoon over the beans and then sprinkle over the crispy kale. Top with the poached eggs, sprinkle with the pumpkin seeds and serve.

SOUPS

SOUP OF ISRAEL

CHILLED RHUBARB AND STRAWBERRY SOUP

BEEF BROTH WITH HERBS AND MEATBALLS

LETTUCE SOUP

OVEN-BAKED LENTIL SOUP WITH GREENS

SOUP OF ISRAEL

Serves 4-6

I love to eat this hearty soup for lunch, with some bread and cheese. It is a perfect early spring soup, inspired by my travels to Israel and the simple soups made by my friends Lior and Ayala, who live in Jerusalem. They have taken over the garden square that they share with neighbours, where they grow a mix of fruit, vegetables and flowers. As with many soups, the vegetables can be changed with the season, to make the most of whatever is plentiful and delicious at the time.

Heat the oil in a large pan over medium heat, add the leek, garlic, salt and some pepper and cook the vegetables gently for 5–10 minutes until they start to release their juices. Add the carrots, celeriac (celery root), potatoes, tomatoes, chickpeas and bay leaf and cook for another 5 minutes.

Add the stock (broth), bring up to a simmer and cook for 30–40 minutes until the vegetables are tender. Do this with the lid off, so the soup reduces slightly and the flavours are concentrated.

Remove from the heat, add the lemon juice and parsley and season to taste with salt and pepper.

PREPARATION: 15 minutes
COOKING: 40–55 minutes

2 tablespoons olive oil
1 large leek, trimmed and cut into
   1-cm/½-inch slices
2 cloves garlic, crushed (minced)
1 teaspoon coarse (kosher) sea salt
3 carrots, trimmed, scrubbed and
   diced
1 celeriac (celery root), peeled and
   diced, and the leaves (if you have
   them) finely chopped
2 potatoes, scrubbed and diced
3 large tomatoes, diced
2 x 400-g/14-oz cans chickpeas,
   drained and rinsed
1 bay leaf
1.2 litres/2 pints (5 cups) vegetable
   stock (broth)
juice of 1 lemon
25 g/1 oz (½ cup) chopped flat-leaf
   parsley
pepper

CHILLED RHUBARB AND STRAWBERRY SOUP

Serves 4-6

This recipe was developed by Andrew Walker, who volunteers in the garden at Great Dixter and also helps me out in the kitchen when I am cooking for students on our study days. Not only is Andrew great company and very entertaining, he is also a skilful and imaginative cook, always looking for new ideas and flavour combinations. This soup, with its clever balance of fruity, sweet and savoury, is a perfect example. I think it makes the ideal starter (appetizer) for a summer Sunday lunch, before, say, a herby roast chicken with a few new potatoes and a big green salad.

Put the rhubarb, star anise and orange juice into a large pan and bring to a boil, then reduce the heat and simmer, covered, for 8-10 minutes until the fruit is soft. Remove from the heat and let cool.

Remove and discard the star anise, then add the strawberries. Transfer the mixture to a blender and blend until smooth or use an immersion blender to blend the mixture. Add the chicken stock (broth) and blend again. Season with the sugar and salt, tasting carefully as you go – add the sugar a little at a time, rather than all in one go. Chill in the refrigerator.

To serve, spoon the chilled soup into bowls and garnish with a swirl of cream, if desired, and a little chopped tarragon.

PREPARATION: 15 minutes,
 plus cooling and chilling
COOKING: 15 minutes

450 g/1 lb (about 9 stalks) forced pink rhubarb, trimmed, washed and coarsely chopped
3 star anise
250 ml/8 fl oz (1 cup) orange juice
225 g/8 oz strawberries, hulled (1½ cups prepared)
475 ml/16 fl oz (2 cups) cold light chicken stock (broth)
50 g/2 oz (¼ cup) caster (superfine) sugar, or to taste
salt

TO GARNISH
single (light) cream (optional)
chopped tarragon leaves

BEEF BROTH WITH HERBS AND MEATBALLS

Serves 5–6/Makes about 1.5 litres/2½ pints (6¼ cups) broth

My good friend Kate Gatacre is an excellent vegetable gardener, and this is her recipe. As Kate says, 'Bone broth is something that is talked about as though it has just been invented by one of those clean-eating cookery writers. Of course, it is, in fact, one of the oldest recipes in the world. It's the perfect recovery food for pretty much any illness, and this is how I make mine. The accoutrements are up to the individual, but this is a traditional Dutch way of turning a clear beef broth into a little more of a meal. Even adding just a few chopped herbs can transform a clear beef broth into something special, though.'

Preheat the oven to 230°C/450°F/Gas Mark 8 (or to its hottest possible setting).

Place the bones, beef shin (shank), carrots and onion into a really large roasting pan and spread out over the bottom of the pan. Roast for 40 minutes, turning everything over halfway through the cooking time, or until the bones and vegetables have got a good browning.

Lift the bones and vegetables into a large pan (at least 6–7 litres/10–12 pints in capacity) and pour away the excess fat from the roasting pan. To deglaze the roasting pan, add a splash of water to the pan and scrape the bottom of the pan with a wooden spatula to release all the caramelized bits and pieces.

PREPARATION: 20 minutes,
 plus chilling overnight
COOKING: 7-9 hours

1.5–2 kg/3¼–4½ lb beef marrow
 bones or veal bones, cut into
 short pieces (a butcher will help
 you with this)
500 g/1 lb 2 oz beef shin (shank),
 cut into slices
2 large carrots, thickly sliced
1 large onion, halved and thickly
 sliced
4 leeks, trimmed and thickly sliced
2 celery stalks, cut into 5-cm/2-inch
 pieces
1 teaspoon salt
1 teaspoon cracked black
 peppercorns
4 bay leaves
450 g/1 lb lean minced (ground)
 beef
small handful mixed herb leaves
 (tarragon, flat-leaf parsley, chives,
 chervil)
crusty bread, to serve (optional)

Pour the liquid from the deglazed roasting pan into the pan with the bones and vegetables and add 3 litres/5 pints (12⅔ cups) cold water, the leeks, celery, salt, peppercorns and bay leaves and bring to a very gentle simmer (you want the occasional bubble rising to the surface, rather than a proper simmer). Part-cover the pan and cook at the same temperature for 6–8 hours, skimming any fat from the surface of the broth now and then as it rises to the surface. As long as it doesn't boil, you shouldn't need to clarify your broth.

Remove the pan from the heat and let cool slightly. Using a slotted spoon, lift out the bones and as many of the vegetables as you can and discard. Strain the broth through a large, muslin (cheesecloth)-lined sieve into a clean pan. If you can, chill overnight, then remove any solidified fat from the surface of the broth. At this stage, you can chill or freeze the broth until needed.

Just before you are ready to serve, put the minced (ground) beef into a bowl, season lightly with salt and pepper and mix well. Roll the mixture into approximately 54 small balls, each a tiny bit bigger than your thumbnail. Put the broth into a clean pan and bring to a gentle simmer. Add the meatballs and simmer for 2–3 minutes until they are just cooked through.

Ladle the broth into warmed soup plates, dividing the meatballs equally among the bowls, and sprinkle over the herbs. Serve with crusty bread, if desired.

Any leftover bone broth can be frozen and used for soups, risottos or stews.

LETTUCE SOUP

Serves 4

This is a wonderful way of using up the outer leaves and ribs of lettuce that might not otherwise make it into the salad bowl. It is also very flexible – use rocket (arugula), spinach, parsley, chervil or whatever salad leaves (greens) and herbs you have to hand, or any combination of them that appeals. This is a great simple lunch but also makes an elegant starter (appetizer) – it would be perfect before a fish dish.

Melt the butter in a heavy pan. Add the onion and cook gently over low heat until thoroughly softened – about 8 minutes. Don't skimp on this step – the onion must be mellow and sweet or it will fight with the relatively delicate flavours of the salad leaves (greens) and herbs.

Add the potato, season with salt and pepper and stir to coat in the melted butter. Add the stock (broth), bring up to a simmer, cover and cook until the potato is soft – about 15 minutes.

Add the lettuce (and herbs, if using), bring the soup back to a simmer and cook for 1 minute, or until all wilted down. Use an immersion blender to blend the soup until smooth. Season to taste with salt and pepper. Ladle the soup into warmed soup plates and garnish with freshly picked herbs.

PREPARATION: 10 minutes
COOKING: 30 minutes

40 g/1½ oz (3 tablespoons) butter
1 onion, finely chopped
1 potato (about 200 g/7 oz), peeled and diced
600 ml/1 pint (2½ cups) vegetable or chicken stock (broth)
4 handfuls (about 300 g/11 oz) lettuce (or mixed salad leaves/greens and herbs, such as basil, parsley, chervil, rocket/arugula), washed, dried and coarsely chopped
salt and pepper
freshly picked herbs, to garnish

OVEN-BAKED LENTIL SOUP WITH GREENS

Serves 6–8

My dear friend Linda Smith lives in Memphis, where she has the most wonderful farm filled with hummingbirds. This soup is one of hers, and is just the sort of thing I want to eat in autumn and winter. In fact, I often make myself a big batch and then eat it for lunch throughout the week; the flavours will deepen the longer it is left. It's simple, delicious and endlessly versatile. I am always adding different things to it depending on my mood and the season – kale, Swiss chard or perpetual spinach, or even parsley (stems and all) are all great additions. And if I feel that I am really in need of something wholesome and reviving, I will pop in a few skinless chicken thighs too. By the time the soup is cooked the meat will be soft enough to eat with a spoon, and the bones will have added lots of flavour to the soup.

Preheat the oven to 180°C/350°F/Gas Mark 4.

Put the stock (broth), dried peas and lentils, vegetables, bay leaves, cumin, salt and pepper into a large heavy casserole dish (Dutch oven) and stir to combine. Cover and bake in the oven for 1 hour, or until the peas and lentils are tender.

Remove from the oven and fish out and discard the bay leaves. Stir through the seasonal greens until wilted. Just before serving, garnish with chopped herbs, then ladle the soup into warmed soup plates and serve with bread and butter, if desired.

PREPARATION: 10 minutes
COOKING: 1 hour

2 litres/3½ pints (8 cups) chicken stock (broth) (or you could use vegetable stock/broth)
225 g/8 oz (1¼ cups) dried yellow split peas
225 g/8 oz (1¼ cups) dried green or brown lentils
4 carrots (about 450 g/1 lb), scrubbed, trimmed and chopped into 2.5-cm/1-inch pieces
4 celery stalks, chopped into 2.5-cm/1-inch pieces
1 leek, trimmed and chopped into 2.5-cm/1-inch pieces
2 bay leaves
1½ teaspoons ground cumin
½ teaspoon salt
1 teaspoon pepper
large bunch seasonal greens (about 250 g/9 oz), stripped away from any large stems, then sliced
chopped herbs, to garnish
crusty bread and butter, to serve (optional)

MAINS

CREAMED CHICKEN

STUFFED SQUASH WITH SPICED MINCE

HADDOCK SOUFFLÉS

PAPER-BAKED TROUT WITH HERBS

STUFFED ARTICHOKES

WARM SPICED LENTILS WITH CAVOLO NERO

PASTA WITH CONTAINER GARDEN SAUCE

FENNEL, AUBERGINE AND ARTICHOKE CAPONATA

PEA SHOOT RISOTTO

CREAMED CHICKEN

Serves 4

This recipe was born one summer weekend when my friend Elizabeth Metcalfe was visiting. After a day of swimming and working up our appetites, we went out into the garden to pick vegetables and herbs for supper and made up this recipe. This is a perfect example of how a few simple ingredients can combine to create something that is far greater than the sum of its parts. The important thing is to allow plenty of time first to brown the chicken, and then for the cream and wine to reduce, as this will really intensify the flavour of the herbs. Elizabeth went home and made it again the next evening for her partner Charlie. Use a good heavy pan that can sit on the stove and go into the oven. I like to serve this with green vegetables and some new potatoes, so that I can crush them into the cream.

PREPARATION: 20 minutes
COOKING: 1¼ hours

1 tablespoon olive oil
25 g/1 oz (2 tablespoons) butter
8 chicken thighs
handful green herbs (parsley, tarragon, chervil and lovage will all work beautifully, but if using lovage, go easy as the flavour is so strong), coarsely chopped, plus extra to garnish
thyme sprig
300 ml/10½ fl oz (1¼ cups) double (heavy) cream
600 ml/1 pint (2½ cups) white wine
salt and pepper

Preheat the oven to 200°C/400°F/Gas Mark 6.

Heat the oil and butter in a heavy ovenproof frying pan or skillet over medium heat. Add the chicken thighs, skin-side down, and pan-fry for about 15 minutes, turning them once, until they are well browned all over, otherwise your finished dish will look pale and sickly.

Place the herbs on top of the chicken and then pour over the cream and wine. Season with salt and pepper. Bake in the oven, uncovered, for 1 hour – it's important to do this without a lid so the sauce can reduce; the finished sauce should have a custard-like consistency. Serve garnished with extra chopped green herbs.

STUFFED SQUASH WITH SPICED MINCE

Serves 4

This dish for me is redolent of childhood winters in New Zealand, when my father would cook it for us in our coal-range oven. I do think sweet flavours like these need a little spice to bring them to life. I like to intensify the flavours by heating the spices in the oil before adding any other ingredients, a technique I learned in India and now use in all my spiced dishes. The coconut oil is my addition to my ·father's recipe – it brings another element of flavour, and really seems to complement the spices.

Preheat the oven to 220°C/425°F/Gas Mark 7.

Cut the squashes in half lengthwise, scoop out and discard the seeds and then open up the cavity along the length of the squashes a little more, leaving a wall of at least 2.5 cm/ 1 inch. Brush the cut sides with olive oil and then place them, cut-sides up, in a roasting pan. Bake for 40 minutes, or until tender.

Meanwhile, heat the coconut oil in a large frying pan or skillet over medium heat. Add the spices and when they start to sizzle add the leek, followed by the beef. Cook, stirring, until the beef is no longer pink. Drain and discard any excess fat. Season with ½ teaspoon salt and a pinch of pepper, then add the tomatoes and parsley and cook for 5–6 minutes, stirring, until the mixture is hot and bubbly.

Remove the baked butternut squashes from the oven. Scoop the beef mixture into the cavities of the baked squash shells and sprinkle with the cheese. Return the stuffed squashes to the oven and bake for 10 minutes, or until the cheese has just melted and is lightly browned.

PREPARATION: 20 minutes
COOKING: 50 minutes

2 butternut squash (about 850 g/ 1 lb 14 oz each)
olive oil, for brushing
2 tablespoons coconut oil
½ teaspoon cumin seeds
½ teaspoon ground turmeric
½ teaspoon caraway seeds
½ teaspoon ground cinnamon
50 g/2 oz (½ cup) chopped leek
450 g/1 lb lean minced (ground) beef
1 x 400-g/14-oz can chopped tomatoes, drained
2 tablespoons chopped flat-leaf parsley
125 g/4½ oz (1 cup) grated Cheddar cheese
salt and pepper

HADDOCK SOUFFLÉS

Serves 4

This recipe is inspired by and dedicated to my great friend Linda Cobb. The great thing about using smoked haddock rather than the ubiquitous cheese is that the salty, smoky flavour really helps to balance out the creamy richness and also makes the soufflés much more satisfying.

Preheat the oven to 190°C/375°F/Gas Mark 5. Grease 4 ramekins (they should be 10 cm/4 inches across and 6 cm/ 2½ inches deep) with melted butter. Use 4 tablespoons of the cheese to coat the insides of the ramekins.

Melt the butter in a pan over medium heat, then stir in the flour and cook for 1 minute, stirring. Start adding the milk, stirring the whole time until you have a smooth, thickish béchamel sauce. Let cool slightly.

Put the egg yolks into a large bowl and beat lightly with a fork. Stir in the thyme, béchamel sauce and some salt and pepper to taste. Set aside to cool to room temperature.

Put the haddock into a pan with the cream and set over medium heat. Once the cream comes to boiling point, reduce the heat and simmer very gently for 2–4 minutes, depending on the thickness of the fillet, until the fish is cooked through. Remove the fish from the cream, set aside on a plate and let cool a little. When the fish is cool enough to handle, remove the skin and flake the fish, removing any bones as you go.

Return the pan of cream to the heat and simmer for another 4 minutes, or until reduced to about 4 tablespoons. Return the fish to the warm cream. Stir the haddock cream and remaining cheese into the béchamel mixture.

In a clean bowl, whisk the egg whites to soft peaks. Gently fold one-third of the beaten egg whites into the béchamel mixture, to lighten it, then gently fold in the remainder. Divide the mixture between the prepared ramekins and put them into a small roasting pan. Add enough boiling water to the roasting pan to come halfway up the sides of the ramekins. Bake in the oven for 14–15 minutes until the soufflés are well risen, golden brown and lightly cooked through. Serve with a green herby salad.

PREPARATION: 15 minutes,
  plus cooling
COOKING: 30 minutes

25 g/1 oz (2 tablespoons) butter,
  plus extra melted butter for
  greasing
120 g/4 oz (1 cup) finely grated
  Gruyère cheese
25 g/1 oz (3 tablespoons) plain
  (all-purpose) flour
400 ml/14 fl oz (1⅔ cups) milk,
  warmed
5 medium (US large) eggs,
  separated
1 teaspoon thyme leaves, finely
  chopped
1 x 130 g/4½ oz piece undyed
  smoked haddock fillet
200 ml/7 fl oz (scant 1 cup)
  double (heavy) cream
salt and pepper
green herby salad, to serve

PAPER-BAKED TROUT WITH HERBS

Serves 4

My bread-making teacher, Phil Harrison, shared this recipe with me. This is a great way to cook trout; wrapping the fish in newspaper stops it drying out, and when you open the parcel, the skin will come away neatly along with the paper. You can adapt this recipe throughout the year, using whichever herbs happen to be at their peak at the time.

PREPARATION: 15 minutes
COOKING: 25 minutes

4 x 350-g/12-oz rainbow trout
   (or brown trout if you are lucky
   enough to get hold of them),
   gutted and cleaned but with tail
   and head intact
herbs (lemon thyme, parsley, dill
   and fennel tops all work well)
lemon slices
salt and pepper

Preheat the oven to 190°C/375°F/Gas Mark 5.

Wash the trout thoroughly and dry the inside of each fish with paper towels but leave the outside moist. Lightly season with salt and pepper inside the gut cavity, then fill the cavity of each fish with a handful of fresh herbs and a few halved lemon slices.

For each trout, you will need one double-page sheet of a tabloid newspaper. Lay the sheet in portrait mode and place the fish near the bottom of the page, with the open side towards you. Take the bottom of the sheet and wrap it up over the open side and fold in the sides so that they align with the length of the fish. Roll the fish up carefully in the paper. If the paper tears too much and you can see the fish through the wrap, start again. You may want to put a small arrow on the head end of each package to remind you on which side of the package the gut cavity is.

Place the wrapped fish side by side on a baking sheet and bake for about 25 minutes (times will vary slightly depending on the size of your fish).

Once baked, put each wrapped fish on a plate. With a pair of scissors, cut the newspaper package open along the gut cavity side of the fish and then make cuts up towards the gills and across the bottom of tail. Take hold of the cut paper and the skin of the fish and gently peel back so that the flesh is exposed, and the head and the tail remain wrapped. If the skin does not peel away from the fish easily, return the wrapped fish to the oven for 5 minutes more, then try again. (If there was too much water in the envelope when you baked it, be prepared with a paper towel to mop up any excess.)

Mains

STUFFED ARTICHOKES

Serves 6

I have my good friend Juliet Roberts to thank for this recipe, which comes originally from her Slovenian lodger. I like to serve these stuffed artichokes with polenta (cornmeal) and mixed salad leaves (greens).

PREPARATION: 20 minutes
COOKING: 30–35 minutes

6 large globe artichokes
juice of 1 lemon
100 g/3½ oz (1 cup) dried
 breadcrumbs (preferably made
 with sourdough bread)
4 cloves garlic, finely chopped
good handful flat-leaf parsley,
 chopped
100 ml/3½ fl oz (scant ½ cup) white
 wine
good glug (1–2 tablespoons) of
 olive oil
200 g/7 oz podded (shelled) broad
 (fava) beans (½ cup prepared)
200 g/7 oz podded (shelled) peas
 (½ cup prepared)
salt and pepper

Wash the artichokes and remove the stems – you're trying to create a stable bottom so they can stand up when you put them in the pan. Slice about 2.5 cm/1 inch off the top of each artichoke, then use a spoon to scoop out its hairy choke.

Put the artichokes into a large pan of water with half the lemon juice. Bring to a boil, then reduce the heat and simmer for 7–10 minutes for younger chokes, longer for older ones. Test for doneness with a fork: the choke should be firm but soft. Drain. (The cooking liquid is useful as a base for stock/broth or can be drunk for its health benefits.)

Meanwhile, prepare the filling. Put the breadcrumbs, garlic and parsley in a bowl with the wine, oil and the remaining lemon juice. Season well with salt and pepper and mix together thoroughly.

Place the artichokes upright in a shallow pan, making sure they are packed in snugly. Stuff the breadcrumb mix in between the leaves and also between the chokes themselves, packing it down.

Blanch the broad (fava) beans in a separate pan of boiling water for 3 minutes, then drain. When they are cool enough to handle, slip off the outer skins and mix with the peas. Stuff the bean and pea mixture in and around the artichokes.

Half-fill the pan with water (so the artichokes are half-immersed) and place over low heat. Partially cover the pan and simmer for about 20 minutes, checking regularly that there is enough water that the chokes don't burn. The breadcrumbs will absorb the water, while the beans and peas steam.

Preheat the grill (broiler) to high. Using a slotted spoon, transfer the artichokes to a heatproof dish and grill for 10 minutes, or until the breadcrumbs are lightly browned.

Mains

WARM SPICED LENTILS WITH CAVOLO NERO

Serves 4 as a main course, 6–8 as a side dish

This is such a versatile dish, and one that really makes the most of the intense, slightly bitter flavour of cavolo nero (Tuscan kale). It is quite unusual to see these earthy ingredients combined with exotic spices, but it really does work. I like this as a main course, but you can also use it as a side dish to accompany lamb, chicken, sausages or even a substantial fish such as sea bass. I use puy (French green) lentils for their nutty flavour and excellent firm texture – the little gleaming dark greeny-grey pebbles look so beautiful with the black leaves of the kale. Make this with vegetable stock (broth) if you prefer, for a completely vegetarian dish.

Heat the oil in a pan over low heat, add the leek, celery, garlic, turmeric and cardamom and cook for about 10 minutes until soft. Add the lentils, stock (broth) and salt, bring to a boil, then reduce the heat and simmer, covered, for 20 minutes.

Uncover the pan and stir through the cavolo nero (Tuscan kale). Simmer, uncovered, for 10 minutes, stirring gently now and then, so as not to break up the lentils.

Remove from the heat, add the lemon juice and stir through the mustard and parsley or coriander (cilantro).

Serve warm, with a good dollop of yogurt and garnish with some extra herbs.

PREPARATION: 10 minutes
COOKING: 40 minutes

2 tablespoons coconut oil
1 large leek, trimmed and diced
1 large celery stalk, finely chopped
2 cloves garlic, very finely chopped, grated or crushed (minced)
1 teaspoon ground turmeric
the seeds from 1 teaspoon cardamom pods, lightly crushed
400 g/14 oz (2 cups) dried puy (French green) lentils
1 litre/1¾ pints (4¼ cups) chicken stock (broth)
1 teaspoon salt
1 x 200-g/7-oz bunch cavolo nero (Tuscan kale), large stems removed and leaves sliced (1¾ cups prepared)
juice of 1 lemon
1 tablespoon mild wholegrain mustard
handful flat-leaf parsley or coriander (cilantro), finely chopped, plus a few whole leaves to garnish
yogurt, to serve

PASTA WITH CONTAINER GARDEN SAUCE

Serves 4

This recipe comes to me from my friend Bill Thomas, the director of Chanticleer Garden just outside Philadelphia. I often stay with him when visiting the gardens there – a real treat, as he is such an interesting cook. The great thing about this sauce is its simplicity. The heat of the pasta is enough to really bring out the flavours of the tomatoes and herbs, without losing any of their freshness and intensity.

Bring a large pan of well-salted water to the boil and cook the pasta for 10 minutes, or until *al dente*.

Meanwhile, make the raw sauce (you can also prepare this sauce a few hours in advance and keep at room temperature). Pound together the basil, parsley, garlic and pine nuts and season with salt and pepper – I do it with a pestle and mortar, but you can use a food processor if you prefer. Either way, be careful not to overdo it – you want a sauce with distinct ingredients, not a purée. Mix in the tomatoes and lightly smash, then stir in the oil.

Drain the pasta, retaining a cup of the cooking water. Mix the pasta and sauce together, adding a little of the reserved cooking water if it seems a little too dry. Serve with the grated cheese in a bowl alongside to sprinkle over.

PREPARATION: 20 minutes
COOKING: 10 minutes

450 g/1 lb dried spaghetti
or linguine
50 g/2 oz (2 cups) basil leaves
50 g/2 oz (1 cup) flat-leaf parsley
leaves
2 cloves garlic
3 tablespoons lightly toasted
pine nuts
350 g/12 oz (2⅓ cups) perfectly
ripe cherry tomatoes, halved
120 ml/4 fl oz (½ cup) good-quality
extra virgin olive oil
salt and pepper
grated pecorino or Parmesan
cheese, to serve

FENNEL, AUBERGINE AND ARTICHOKE CAPONATA

Serves 4

Caponata is a Sicilian dish, but for me it is a reminder of Israel. It is exactly the kind of thing I put together when cooking with my friends Lior and Ayala in Jerusalem. Like me, they are interested in bringing different flavours together and in making the most of whatever is in season. We often go to the market just before the beginning of Shabbat to pick up whatever has not sold. It is a great test of culinary ingenuity! You can make this versatile dish with fresh vegetables if you have them, or preserved if you don't, and serve it as a vegetarian main course with some good bread, for lunch with an egg on top or as a side dish to accompany any roasted or grilled (broiled) meat or fish.

PREPARATION: 20 minutes
COOKING: 25 minutes

4 tablespoons rapeseed (canola) oil
½ onion, finely chopped
4 globe artichokes (or 200 g/7 oz prepared artichoke hearts in olive oil, drained)
lemon juice, to prevent discolouration (if using fresh artichokes)
2 cloves garlic, finely chopped
2 spring onions (scallions), chopped
1 small fennel bulb, trimmed and thinly sliced
1 aubergine (eggplant), peeled using a vegetable peeler, then cut into 1.5-cm/¾-inch dice
3 tomatoes, diced
4 tablespoons canned chopped tomatoes
4 tablespoons red wine vinegar
2 tablespoons capers, drained and rinsed
2 tablespoons toasted pumpkin seeds
1 tablespoon finely chopped basil
1 tablespoon finely chopped flat-leaf parsley
1 tablespoon finely chopped lemon thyme
salt and pepper
toasted bread, to serve

Heat the oil in a large frying pan or skillet over medium heat. Add the onion, cover and leave for 10 minutes to sweat down, stirring every so often.

Meanwhile, prepare the globe artichokes, if using. Remove the leaves until only the innermost leaves and hearts remain. (You can keep the outer leaves to steam and then eat with vinaigrette or aioli – delicious.) Trim the stems and hard leaf remnants around the bottoms, and use a vegetable peeler to peel the stems, removing the tough exterior. Chop the hearts in half and use a spoon to remove the hairy chokes. Cut in half again so you are left with quarters of artichoke heart. If you are not using them immediately, rub with a little lemon juice to stop discolouration.

Add the garlic, spring onions (scallions), fennel, aubergine (eggplant), tomatoes (fresh and canned), artichoke hearts, vinegar, capers and pumpkin seeds to the frying pan with the onion, cover and simmer for 10 minutes, or until all the vegetables are tender but not too soft.

Add the herbs and cook, uncovered, for another 5 minutes to allow the flavours to combine. Season with salt and pepper and serve warm or at room temperature, spooned over toasted bread.

Mains

PEA SHOOT RISOTTO

Serves 4

Where possible, I do like to try to make use of more than one part of the plants I'm growing. Pea shoots are a particular favourite for their beauty and their excellent flavour. I have my great friend and travelling companion Lee Hallman to thank for this recipe. Lee lives in Fort Worth, Texas, where she has a wonderful container garden. This risotto is a real taste of early summer, and a great way to show off tender young vegetables at their best. You could also use young broad (fava) beans and broad bean tops (greens), either in addition to or instead of the peas. This is delicious with a lightly seasoned baby leaf (greens) salad, dressed simply with olive oil.

PREPARATION: 15 minutes
COOKING: 30 minutes

1 tablespoon vegetable oil
piece of butter
5 spring onions (scallions), finely chopped
50 g/2 oz (½ cup) pea shoots
300 g/11 oz (1½ cups) risotto rice
1.2 litres/2 pints (5 cups) warm vegetable stock (broth)
100 g/3½ oz (1½ cups) sugar snap peas, halved on the diagonal if large
30 g/1¼ oz (⅓ cup) grated Parmesan cheese, plus extra for serving
1 tablespoon crème fraîche
salt and pepper

Heat the oil and butter in a pan over medium heat, add the spring onions (scallions) and cook for about 2 minutes until translucent.

Meanwhile, finely chop the pea shoots, reserving a few whole pea shoots for a garnish if desired.

Add the risotto rice to the pan and cook gently for 2 minutes, stirring all the time, without colouring. Add a ladleful of stock (broth), stir through and continue cooking at a gentle bubble until the liquid has been absorbed. Repeat the process, gradually adding the stock a ladleful at a time until about two-thirds of the stock has been used – this will take about 20 minutes.

At this point, add the sugar snap peas, then continue adding the stock, a ladleful at a time, until it is all used up – this will take about 5 minutes more. The rice should be cooked through but still retain a slight bite to it.

Stir in the Parmesan, crème fraîche and chopped pea shoots and season with salt and pepper to taste. Serve garnished with the reserved pea shoots, if using, and extra Parmesan to sprinkle over.

SALADS & SIDE DISHES

FIGS WITH GOAT'S CURD AND ROCKET

BAKED BEETROOT SALAD

PEA AND POTATO SALAD

MAURITIAN SLAW

SHAVED FENNEL AND APPLE SALAD
WITH SMOKED MACKEREL

COURGETTE SALAD WITH ANCHOVIES AND CAPERS

THREE GREAT MIDDLE EASTERN SALADS

LEBANESE BROAD BEANS

BEETROOT HUMMUS

GRILLED SUMMER VEGETABLES WITH FETA

CREAMED SWISS CHARD

SEA KALE WITH BAGNA CAUDA

PEAS AND PEA SHOOTS WITH SPRING ONIONS
AND MINT

TEMPURA BABY COURGETTES

FIGS WITH GOAT'S CURD AND ROCKET

Serves 2 as a light lunch, or 4 as a starter (appetizer)

If, like me, you are a fig pig then you are going to love this one. I remember the first time I was out in the desert in Israel and found a fig tree that had ripe fruit on it. It was like nothing I had ever tasted before. While I can't quite replicate those conditions here in Sussex, it is still possible to grow good figs, provided you can give them a sheltered spot and a bit of sunshine. Fig trees like to have their roots confined, which makes them perfect for container growing. This recipe comes from one of the people who inspired this book, Cornelia Steffen (see page 13). She has one of the best container gardens I have ever seen, but of course I wouldn't dream of telling her that to her face. This makes a wonderful starter (appetizer) or light lunch.

PREPARATION: 10 minutes

4 ripe figs, quartered

4 mint sprigs, leaves torn

200 g/7 oz (10 cups) baby rocket (arugula) leaves

3 tablespoons plus 1 teaspoon extra virgin olive oil

3 tablespoons plus 1 teaspoon lemon juice

1 teaspoon Dijon mustard

200 g/7 oz goat's curd (or you can use fresh soft goat's cheese)

salt and pepper

Put the figs, mint and rocket (arugula) in a serving bowl.

To make a dressing, whisk together the oil, lemon juice and mustard in a small bowl and season with salt and pepper.

Drizzle the dressing over the mint and rocket and toss gently to combine. Top with the figs and goat's curd and season with pepper.

BAKED BEETROOT SALAD

Serves 4

My sister Lisa has the same love for beetroot as I do. Lisa is not a gardener and has no interest in taking it on, but her husband loves to grow vegetables with their three children. Beetroot (beet) is something that does well for them, so they are always looking for new ways to use it in the kitchen. This recipe is typical of their style of cooking: simple, fresh and designed to show the vegetables off at their best. Toasting the hazelnuts will give a more intense flavour; leaving them raw gives a fresher taste.

Preheat the oven to 200°C/400°F/Gas Mark 6.

In a bowl, toss the beetroot (beets) in 1 tablespoon each of the oil and vinegar and season with salt and pepper. Spread the beetroot over the bottom of an ovenproof dish or small roasting pan, cover tightly with aluminium foil and roast for 30 minutes, or until almost tender.

While the beetroot is cooking, bring a pan of salted water to the boil, add the green beans and cook for no more than a minute or two until only just tender. Drain, then add to the beetroot and continue to roast for another 5 minutes.

While the vegetables are roasting, make the dressing by whisking the remaining oil and vinegar together with some seasoning to taste. Put the rocket (arugula) in a bowl and coat with a little of the dressing.

To assemble the salad, arrange the rocket over a large serving platter. Sprinkle over the roasted vegetables, goat's cheese and hazelnuts. Drizzle over the remaining dressing and then sprinkle over the mint leaves and a few sea salt flakes.

PREPARATION: 15 minutes
COOKING: 35 minutes

500 g/1 lb 2 oz (about 6) raw beetroot (beets), peeled and cut into wedges
3 tablespoons rapeseed (canola) oil
3 tablespoons balsamic vinegar
400 g/14 oz fine green beans, trimmed
150 g/5 oz (7½ cups) rocket (arugula)
120 g/4 oz goat's cheese (ideally cylinder shaped), thinly sliced
50 g/2 oz (⅓ cup) toasted skinned hazelnuts, coarsely chopped
small handful baby mint leaves
salt and pepper

PEA AND POTATO SALAD

Serves 6

Mickel Folcarelli, who gave me this recipe, is another gardener who loves to cook, so we always have a lot to talk about. This dish puts freshly dug potatoes centre stage, which to my mind is exactly where they deserve to be. I never tire of going outside to rummage in the container and see what is there – it's rather like opening a gift. There are so many salad (waxy) potatoes on the market, but my longstanding favourite is 'Charlotte', for its excellent performance, waxy texture and flavour. I know the dressing looks rather heavy on the vinegar, but don't stint – you will need the tanginess to cut through the richness of the mayonnaise. I like to add a handful of chopped mint to Mickel's original version, just for a little extra freshness. If you want to make the salad more substantial, add quartered hard-boiled eggs just before serving.

PREPARATION: 15 minutes,
   plus standing
COOKING: 15–20 minutes

1 kg/2¼ lb small, even-size salad
   (waxy) potatoes, peeled,
   scrubbed or scraped clean as you
   prefer and halved
2 tablespoons neutral-tasting oil,
   such as rapeseed (canola) or
   sunflower (don't use olive)
4 teaspoons (apple) cider vinegar
½ teaspoon salt
1 teaspoon Dijon mustard
2 teaspoons celery seeds
150 g/5 oz (1 cup) fresh peas
4 tablespoons mayonnaise – decent
   shop-bought is fine
handful mint leaves, chopped
   (optional)
salt and pepper

Bring a large pan of salted water to the boil. Add the potatoes and cook until soft but not mushy (this will usually take between 10 and 15 minutes depending on their size and how recently they were dug). Drain the potatoes and tip them into a large bowl. Cut into slightly smaller, chunky pieces if they are large.

Whisk together the oil, 2 teaspoons of the vinegar, the salt, mustard and celery seeds, then pour over the hot potatoes. Mix well and let stand either at room temperature or in the refrigerator for at least 2 hours, turning the potatoes now and then so that they evenly absorb the dressing.

Just before you are ready to serve, drop the peas into a pan of boiling salted water and cook for 1–2 minutes until just tender. Drain and refresh under cold running water. Set aside.

Mix together the mayonnaise, the remaining vinegar and the mint, if using, in a small bowl and season to taste with a little salt and pepper.

Pour the mayonnaise mixture over potatoes, add the peas and toss gently.

Salads & Side Dishes

MAURITIAN SLAW

Serves 4–6

The Global Generation's Skip Garden is based in King's Cross, a great part of London that also happens to be home to my wonderful publisher. It serves this colourful and substantial salad in its café alongside pies, quiches and toasted sandwiches. The Skip Garden's version of the classic Mauritian slaw, *achard de légumes*, combines the best seasonal vegetables with the warmth and vibrancy of the East African coast. To vary the flavours of this slaw, you can also add grated fresh ginger to the spices while they are toasting. You can also sprinkle over some toasted desiccated (dried flaked) coconut or pumpkin, sunflower or sesame seeds to add a little more texture and nutty flavour.

PREPARATION: 15 minutes
COOKING: 5 minutes

6 black or curly kale leaves (about 125 g/4½ oz), washed, dried, tough stems and ribs removed and coarsely chopped
a substantial pinch each of salt and caster (superfine) sugar
¼ small red cabbage (about 250 g/ 9 oz), core removed and the rest thinly sliced
2 large carrots (about 350 g/12 oz), washed and coarsely grated
1 teaspoon black mustard seeds
1 teaspoon cumin seeds
1 teaspoon ground coriander
½ teaspoon ground turmeric
1½ teaspoons toasted sesame oil
grated zest and juice of ½ lemon
pepper

Put the kale into a large bowl, add the salt and sugar and massage the ingredients into the leaves for about 30 seconds. Set aside. Combine the shredded red cabbage and grated carrot in another large bowl.

Place a good heavy frying pan or skillet over medium heat. Once the pan is too hot to touch, add the mustard and cumin seeds and cook for about 10 seconds, then add the coriander and turmeric and cook for a few more seconds. You will know the spices are toasted when they release their aromas and the seeds begin to shimmy about in the pan.

Tip the spices straight into the bowl with the carrot and cabbage, then add the kale, oil and lemon zest and juice. Mix well, adjust the seasoning to taste and serve.

SHAVED FENNEL AND APPLE SALAD WITH SMOKED MACKEREL

Serves 2

I love this salad because it brings together some of my favourite ingredients, with a little unexpected twist from the almonds, which bring welcome crunch and a deep toasted flavour. The recipe comes to me from a friend, Isabelle, who is training to be a chef. This dish makes a wonderful light lunch, but you could also serve it as a starter (appetizer), or make it part of a larger spread by adding another couple of salads and some warm bread.

Preheat the oven to 180°C/350°F/Gas Mark 4.

Put the almonds into a small roasting pan with the lemon zest and juice. Place in the oven and roast until the nuts are browned, about 10 minutes. Let cool, then coarsely chop.

Make the vinaigrette. Whisk together the vinegar, lemon juice, mustard, oil and sugar in a small bowl. Season with salt and pepper, and add a little more lemon juice or mustard, to taste.

Put the chopped almonds, fennel, apples, capers, dill and parsley into a bowl. Break up the mackerel fillets into chunks and add to the salad. Pour over the vinaigrette, toss gently and serve.

PREPARATION: 15 minutes, plus cooling
COOKING: 10 minutes

75 g/3 oz (½ cup) whole almonds, with skins on
grated zest and juice of 1 lemon
2 small fennel bulbs, trimmed and thinly sliced
2 apples, cored and diced
1 tablespoon capers, coarsely chopped
1 bunch dill, coarsely chopped
1 bunch flat-leaf parsley, coarsely chopped
175 g/6 oz smoked mackerel fillets

FOR THE VINAIGRETTE
1 tablespoon (apple) cider vinegar
juice of 1 lemon
1–2 tablespoons Dijon mustard
4 tablespoons olive oil
¼ teaspoon sugar
salt and pepper

COURGETTE SALAD WITH ANCHOVIES AND CAPERS

Serves 4

The strong salty flavours of anchovies and capers work brilliantly with the sweetness of courgettes (zucchini) and the mild, milky burrata. I like to eat this for lunch, with some fresh bread, but it would also make a great side dish to accompany my desert island dish, a slow-cooked shoulder of lamb. In that case I would leave out the burrata and perhaps add some feta instead as its salty freshness is the perfect foil for the sweetness of lamb.

PREPARATION: 15 minutes
COOKING: 10 minutes

6 courgettes (zucchini) (about
   1 kg/2¼ lb), halved lengthwise,
   then cut in half widthwise
6 tablespoons rapeseed (canola) oil
4 tablespoons chopped flat-leaf
   parsley
4 anchovy fillets in olive oil, drained
   on paper towels and finely
   chopped
3 tablespoons nonpareille capers,
   drained and rinsed
2 tablespoons lemon juice
200 g/7 oz burrata or buffalo
   mozzarella
salt and pepper

Put the courgettes (zucchini) into a bowl with 2 tablespoons of the oil and some salt and pepper and toss to coat.

Place a large frying pan or skillet over medium–high heat, add a layer of the courgettes, cut-face down, and cook for about 5 minutes, turning over halfway through, until they are golden brown all over and just tender when pierced with a small, sharp knife. Transfer them to a plate and repeat with the remaining courgettes.

Meanwhile, make a dressing by mixing together the parsley, the remaining oil, the anchovies, capers and lemon juice in a bowl and seasoning to taste with salt and pepper.

Return all the courgettes to the hot pan. Add all but one tablespoon of the dressing to the courgettes and turn to coat in the mixture.

Transfer the courgettes to a large serving dish. Tear the burrata or mozzarella into rough chunks, toss with the remaining dressing and dot over the courgettes.

THREE GREAT MIDDLE EASTERN SALADS

In Israel and elsewhere in the Middle East, it is common to have a selection of salads on the table. I really like this way of eating. It's so much more relaxed, and means everyone can help themselves to what they like – great when you are catering for people who like different things. I often serve food this way when I am in Australia cooking for my niece and nephews, Lily, Rico and Kosta. These salads are a great way of showcasing your seasonal vegetables at their best, and will turn simple grilled (broiled) meat or fish into a feast. Just add rice or some good-qualilty bread.

TABBOULEH

Serves 4

Put the bulgar wheat into a large heatproof bowl and cover with plenty of boiling hot water. Let soak for 10 minutes, or until soft, then tip into a sieve and let drain until cold.

Tip the drained bulgar wheat into a bowl and stir in the mint, parsley, spring onions (scallions) or chives, oil, lemon juice and some salt and pepper to taste. Stir in the chopped tomato. Eat the tabbouleh with vine (grape) leaves, or use lettuce leaves to scoop it up.

PREPARATION: 15 minutes,
   plus cooling

200 g/7 oz (1½ cups) medium
   bulgar wheat
15 g/½ oz mint leaves, finely
   chopped (⅓ cup prepared)
100 g/3½ oz flat-leaf parsley leaves,
   finely chopped (2 cups prepared)
1 bunch spring onions (scallions),
   trimmed and finely chopped, or
   25 g/1 oz (½ cup) chopped chives
5 tablespoons extra virgin olive oil
4 tablespoons lemon juice
1 tomato, finely chopped
salt and pepper
vine (grape) leaves or lettuce
   leaves, to serve

BABA GHANOUSH

Serves 4

Preheat the oven to 230°C/450°F/Gas Mark 8 (or to its hottest possible setting).

Put the onions onto a baking sheet and roast for 10 minutes. Using the tines of a fork, pierce the aubergines (eggplants) a few times close to their stems, then add them to the baking sheet and roast for another 30–40 minutes until the aubergines feel soft and squidgy inside. Remove the tray from the oven and let cool.

Peel the onions and coarsely chop the flesh. Halve the aubergines lengthwise, scoop out the flesh onto a board and coarsely chop, discarding the skins.

Coarsely chop the garlic, drop it into a mortar and add the salt. Pound with the pestle into a smooth paste, then add the tahini and lemon juice and mix together well.

Scoop the onions and aubergines into a bowl, add the tahini mixture and mix together until well combined. The baba ghanoush should have a thick consistency. Serve at room temperature, garnished with chopped parsley, if desired.

PREPARATION: 20 minutes, plus cooling
COOKING: 40–50 minutes

2 small onions, unpeeled and left whole
2 large aubergines (eggplants) (about 300 g/11 oz each)
4–5 cloves garlic
1 teaspoon salt
75 g/3 oz (⅓ cup) light tahini
2 tablespoons lemon juice
chopped flat-leaf parsley, to garnish (optional)

ALAYEH (TOMATO SALAD)

Serves 4

Heat the oil in frying pan or skillet over medium heat, add the garlic and, as soon as it starts to sizzle and change colour, add half the onions, half the tomatoes and the stock (broth), paprika and salt. Simmer gently for 4 minutes, stirring now and then.

When all the ingredients are soft, remove from the heat, stir in the brandy and let cool.

When you are ready to serve, stir in the remaining onions and tomatoes. This will give you the most wonderful combination of textures, with the cooked vegetables giving mellow sweetness and the raw ones adding freshness and crunch. Adjust the seasoning to taste and serve cold.

PREPARATION: 10 minutes, plus cooling
COOKING: 5 minutes

1 tablespoon olive oil
6 cloves garlic, finely chopped
3 small onions, finely chopped
450 g/1 lb ripe but firm tomatoes, cut into small dice (2½ cups prepared)
1 tablespoon chicken stock (broth)
1 teaspoon paprika
½ teaspoon salt, or to taste
1 tablespoon brandy

LEBANESE BROAD BEANS

Serves 4

Thomas Gooch is a great friend, and he has done a lot of container gardening in his native Melbourne over the years. Recently I was lucky enough to go and see what he is doing in the yard behind his studio. This is a small area in the middle of the city, and yet it is so productive. It really is a great example of what you can achieve with a little effort. This recipe comes from him and is adapted from something he ate in a market in Melbourne. I like it because it makes use of the whole beans, pods and all. Thomas has experimented with a few different flavourings and reports that broad (fava) beans with sweet paprika works particularly well with rice or fish. But this variation is his favourite. Note the beans must be very young and tender for this to work.

PREPARATION: 10 minutes
COOKING: 25–30 minutes

olive oil, for frying
1 onion, diced
500 g/1 lb 2 oz (4 cups) very
    young and tender broad (fava)
    beans in their pods, trimmed
    and destringed
1 bunch flat-leaf parsley, chopped
1 bunch coriander (cilantro),
    chopped
juice of 1 lemon
salt and pepper

Heat a glug (1–2 tablespoons) of oil in a frying pan or skillet, add the onion and cook over medium heat for 5–10 minutes until translucent and softened.

Chop the beans into pieces about 2.5 cm/1 inch long, then add them to the pan along with another glug of oil. Season with salt and pepper, cover and cook for 10 minutes.

Add the parsley, coriander (cilantro) and lemon juice and cook over low heat for another 10 minutes, stirring occasionally. The beans should still have a little bite to them when they're done.

BEETROOT HUMMUS

Serves 4

Hummus made entirely from chickpeas is one of the great loves of my life, but even I recognize the need to change things up a little from time to time. This recipe is the answer. Not only do you get a new flavour, the colour is incredible too. A dish of this beetroot hummus looks stunning alongside a plate of raw vegetables and will keep you going while you wait for lunch, ideally with a glass of champagne. Note that this is good made with carrots as well. My friend Henry Witheridge – another great gardener – recently introduced me to split pea hummus too. Another exciting addition to the hummus repertoire.

PREPARATION: 10 minutes,
  plus cooling
COOKING: 45–60 minutes

1 large raw beetroot (beet)
  (about 225 g/8 oz)
3 tablespoons olive oil
1 x 400-g/14-oz can chickpeas,
  drained and rinsed
1 tablespoon lemon juice
2 cloves garlic, crushed (minced)
2 tablespoons tahini
salt and pepper
raw vegetables, to serve (optional)

Preheat the oven to 180°C/350°F/Gas Mark 4.

Trim the beetroot (beet) and peel the root. Cut into 3-cm/1¼-inch cubes. Wrap the beetroot cubes in aluminium foil with 1 tablespoon of the oil. Bake for 45–60 minutes until soft, then remove from the aluminium foil, put into a bowl and let cool.

Put the cooled beetroot into a food processor with 1 tablespoon of the oil, the chickpeas, lemon juice, garlic and tahini and process until smooth. Season to taste with salt and pepper. Transfer to a bowl and pour over the remaining oil. Serve with raw vegetables, if desired.

GRILLED SUMMER VEGETABLES WITH FETA

Serves 6

Summer char-grilled vegetables are already pretty close to perfect as far as I am concerned, but this clever dressing really takes them to a whole new level. Isabelle, a talented young trainee chef I know, gave me this recipe. It is great as it is, but you can also serve it with grilled (broiled) fish (sea bass would be perfect) or lamb to make it more substantial.

Heat a large ridged cast-iron griddle (grill) or your barbecue (grill) to a high heat. Brush the vegetables with oil and cook in batches until nicely charred. The corn will take 10–12 minutes, turning occasionally; the courgettes (zucchini) and lettuces about 2 minutes on each side. Season the vegetables lightly with salt and pepper.

To make the dressing, put all the ingredients into a mini food processor and process until smooth. Season with salt and pepper to taste.

To assemble the salad, arrange the char-grilled vegetables attractively on a large serving platter and sprinkle over the feta. Serve with the dressing in a bowl for dipping or drizzle the dressing over the vegetables.

PREPARATION: 10 minutes
COOKING: 25 minutes

6 Little Gem lettuce hearts, halved lengthwise
6 ears of corn, each cut across widthwise into 4 pieces
3 courgettes (zucchini), thickly sliced on the diagonal
olive oil, for grilling
200 g/7 oz feta cheese, crumbled (1⅓ cups prepared)
salt and pepper

FOR THE DRESSING
25 g/1 oz (1 cup) basil leaves
finely grated zest of 2 lemons
3 tablespoons lemon juice
2 teaspoons honey

CREAMED SWISS CHARD

Serves 2

I cannot imagine gardening without Swiss chard. What a tough, good-tempered plant it is, and so handsome grown in a container. It is so productive that sometimes the challenge is to keep coming up with fresh ideas for how to use it. This recipe makes a fantastic accompaniment – try it with roast lamb or chicken. My friend Susan Dyer likes to make a simple side dish by cutting Swiss chard on the bias into 10-cm/ 4-inch long pieces, tossing with olive oil, salt and pepper, then roasting in a hot oven until tender.

PREPARATION: 10 minutes
COOKING: 20 minutes

2 large bunches Swiss chard
   (about 500 g/1 lb 2 oz), washed
   (use both the stalks/stems
   and leaves)
40 g/1½ oz (⅓ cup) flaked
   (slivered) almonds
25 g/1 oz (2 tablespoons) butter
2 spring onions (scallions),
   trimmed and chopped
100 g/3½ oz (½ cup) full-fat
   cream cheese
pinch of freshly grated nutmeg
salt and pepper

Separate the Swiss chard stems from the leaves (greens). Thinly slice the stems across (these take a bit longer to cook), then bunch up the leaves and slice them across into 2.5-cm/ 1-inch strips.

Toast the almonds in a dry frying pan or skillet for 5 minutes, moving them around in the pan to stop them catching and burning. Remove from the heat and reserve 2 tablespoons of the toasted almonds for garnish.

Return the pan with the remaining almonds to the heat, add the butter, then the spring onions (scallions) and Swiss chard stalks, cover and cook for 5 minutes, stirring all the time. Once soft, add the Swiss chard leaves, season with salt and pepper, cover and cook for about 5 minutes until the leaves have wilted and the stalks are tender.

Add the cream cheese to the pan and stir over low heat until it has melted and coated the chard. Season to taste with the nutmeg, salt and pepper.

To serve, transfer to a warmed serving dish and garnish with the reserved toasted almonds.

SEA KALE WITH BAGNA CAUDA

Serves 4-6

The pungent flavour of this simple sauce is perfect with boiled or steamed sea kale or, indeed, most other vegetables, either raw or cooked. It's particularly delicious with chicory (Belgian endive). Try serving this dish as an accompaniment to steak or lamb, or you can even serve it with a selection of raw crudités as a starter (appetizer) before dinner with a glass of something chilled.

PREPARATION: 20 minutes
COOKING: 10 minutes

1-2 handfuls sea kale stems
4 fat cloves garlic, thinly sliced
pinch of salt
12 anchovy fillets (if packed in salt, rinse before using), finely chopped
150 ml/5 fl oz (⅔ cup) olive oil (it doesn't need to be your best extra virgin)
80 g/3 oz (6 tablespoons) cold unsalted butter, diced, plus extra if necessary

Trim the ends of the sea kale, and cut into manageable lengths. Steam the kale for 10 minutes or cook it in a pan of boiling water for about 6 minutes until tender. Drain and then arrange the sea kale on a plate or serving dish.

Meanwhile, make the bagna cauda. Put the garlic into a mortar with the salt and pound with the pestle into a smooth paste. Add the anchovies and pound again until smooth. Scrape the mixture into a small pan, add the oil and warm gently over low heat, stirring occasionally. Remove from the heat and gradually whisk in the butter, a small piece at a time, to produce a smooth emulsified sauce. If the sauce doesn't come together, transfer it to a food processor and process until smooth, gradually adding in an extra 20-30 g/¾-1¼ oz (1½-2 tablespoons) cold unsalted butter, a piece at a time.

Serve the sea kale with the warm sauce in a bowl for dipping.

PEAS AND PEA SHOOTS WITH SPRING ONIONS AND MINT

Serves 4

As with so many of the side dishes in this book, I have applied two criteria: first, it must allow a crop from the container garden to shine; and second, it must be a great accompaniment to lamb. As a child of New Zealand, I feel it is my patriotic duty to eat as much lamb as possible. Just as well I love it so much. If you're not quite such a lamb fanatic, this is also wonderful with roast chicken or chicken thighs baked in the oven with a few handfuls of herbs. I really enjoy cooking with pea shoots. Not only do they look pretty, they are also very intensely flavoured. I find them a little greener and less sweet than the peas.

Bring a large heavy pan of salted water to the boil. Add the peas and cook until they are just tender – about 3 minutes. (If using frozen peas, they will only need 1 minute.) Drain and rinse under cold running water.

Return the pan to the heat and add the oil. Add the spring onions (scallions) and a pinch of salt, cover and cook over moderately low heat, stirring occasionally, for 5 minutes, or until softened.

Stir in the peas, cover and cook for 1 minute, or until heated through. Stir in the butter, 1 tablespoon at a time, then add the pea shoots and stir until wilted. Remove from the heat, stir in the mint and season with salt and pepper to taste.

Serve with pan-fried or grilled (broiled) lamb chops, roast chicken or herby baked chicken thighs.

PREPARATION: 10 minutes
COOKING: 10 minutes

450 g/1 lb (3 cups) fresh or
    frozen peas
1½ tablespoons extra virgin olive oil
3 spring onions (scallions), cut into
    5-mm/¼-inch slices
40 g/1½ oz (3 tablespoons)
    unsalted butter
250 g/9 oz (3 cups) tender pea
    shoots (or small watercress
    sprigs, or a mix of both)
20 g/¾ oz (⅔ cup) mint leaves
    (a small bunch), coarsely
    chopped if large
salt and pepper
pan-fried or grilled (broiled) lamb
    chops or roast chicken, to serve

TEMPURA BABY COURGETTES

Serves 6

I am pleased to see so many people rising to the challenge of dealing with bumper crops of courgettes (zucchini). A special mention must go to David Mattern, the vegetable gardener at Chanticleer, and his friends Jeff and Joe, who have conducted a series of experiments with the aim of finding the best way of cooking with these prolific vegetables. This is their winning recipe. Note this works best with small courgettes, ideally around 10 cm/4 inches long. If their blossoms are still in place, so much the better.

Make the batter by whisking together the flour, cornflour (cornstarch), egg, beer, herbs and a good pinch of salt. It should be slightly thinner than pancake batter.

Pour the oil into a heavy frying pan or skillet to a depth of about 1 cm/½ inch and place over high heat to heat up while you slice the courgettes (zucchini) in half lengthwise. Put the courgettes into a bowl and toss with a little extra flour to coat.

Line a large baking sheet with paper towels. Dip the courgettes in the batter and then carefully lower them into the hot oil – you may need to cook them in batches. Pan-fry until golden brown on both sides – about 2½ minutes. Once cooked, lift the courgettes onto the prepared baking sheet and let drain. Transfer onto a serving plate and sprinkle with salt and a little pepper. Serve with the sour cream and green peppercorns sprinkled on top or in a small bowl as a dip.

PREPARATION: 15 minutes
COOKING: 10 minutes

130 g/4½ oz (1 cup) plain (all-purpose) flour, plus extra for dusting
1 tablespoon cornflour (cornstarch)
1 egg, beaten
250 ml/8 fl oz (1 cup) beer (I use pale ale)
1 teaspoon each of chopped rosemary and thyme
olive oil, for frying
12 small courgettes (zucchini), blossoms still attached if possible
salt and pepper

TO SERVE
sour cream
1 tablespoon brined green peppercorns, drained

CAKES & DESSERTS

TUNISIAN LEMON AND ORANGE CAKE

GOOSEBERRY CAKE

SCENTED-LEAF PELARGONIUM SORBET

FIG LEAF ICE-CREAM

CHOCOLATE MOUSSE WITH ORANGE SALAD

BAKED APRICOTS WITH BAY AND HONEY

BAKED CUSTARD WITH BLUEBERRIES

BAKED APPLES

RHUBARB, ALMOND AND GINGER TART

BLACKCURRANT TART

BASIL PAVLOVA

SUMMER PUDDING

PEACH COBBLER

TUNISIAN LEMON AND ORANGE CAKE

Serves 8

My dear friend Gaye Fox doesn't like desserts very much, but she is kind enough to make them for me when I go to stay with her. This cake is one of my favourites. It works well as a dessert cake, with some crème fraîche alongside, but I think I like it best as a little pick-me-up with a strong black coffee after lunch. You can make this gluten free by cutting out the breadcrumbs and adding more ground almonds (almond meal) instead.

PREPARATION: 20 minutes, plus overnight chilling
COOKING: 50 minutes

2½ tablespoons fresh white breadcrumbs
100 g/3½ oz (1 cup) ground almonds (almond meal)
200 g/7 oz (1 cup) caster (superfine) sugar
1½ teaspoons baking powder
200 ml/7 fl oz (scant 1 cup) sunflower oil, plus extra for greasing
4 eggs
grated zest of 1 orange
grated zest of 1 lemon
candied orange slices, to decorate (optional)

FOR THE SYRUP
100 g/3½ oz (½ cup) caster (superfine) sugar
juice of 1 orange and 2 lemons
4 cloves
1 small cinnamon stick

Grease and then double-line the bottom and sides of a 20-cm/8-inch loose-bottom round cake pan with baking (parchment) paper.

Mix the breadcrumbs, almonds, sugar and baking powder together in a large bowl. Stir in the oil and then the eggs, one at a time. Add the orange and lemon zest and mix well but don't over-beat.

Pour the batter into the prepared pan and place in a cold oven. Turn the oven on to 190°C/375°F/Gas Mark 5 and bake for 50 minutes, or until the cake is a rich brown on top and a skewer inserted into the centre comes out clean. Let cool in the pan for 5 minutes.

Meanwhile, make the syrup. Put all the ingredients into a pan and bring them gently to a boil, stirring until the sugar has dissolved. Reduce the heat and simmer until the mixture has reduced by half (to about 5 tablespoons) and is thick and syrupy. Remove and discard the cinnamon stick.

Run a thin round-bladed (blunt) knife around the edge of the still-warm cake, remove the cake from the pan and carefully peel away the baking (parchment) paper from the sides and bottom. Place the cake on a plate. Use a skewer to pierce holes over the surface of the cake, then pour the syrup over the cake and let stand until the syrup has all soaked in. Decorate with the candied orange slices, if using.

Once the cake is cool, loosely cover with clingfilm (plastic wrap) and place in the refrigerator overnight before serving.

GOOSEBERRY CAKE

Serves 8

Rosemary Alexander, the creator of the English Gardening School, is very much a hands-on gardener and designer, and also a great cook. I just wish she gardened – and cooked – a bit closer to me. This wonderful recipe comes from Rosemary. The moisture and flavour from the fresh gooseberries really bring the cake to life and stop it from being dull and cloying. The end result is somewhere between a dessert and a cake, so perfect either to finish a meal or with morning coffee or afternoon tea. This recipe is a brilliant way of making use of a small harvest. If you only have a handful or so of gooseberries, bake this cake.

PREPARATION: 10 minutes, plus cooling
COOKING: 45 minutes

200 g/7 oz (1⅓ cups) gooseberries, trimmed
2 tablespoons runny honey
1 tablespoon elderflower cordial (syrup) (optional)
150 g/5 oz (¾ cup) caster (superfine) sugar
150 g/5 oz (1¼ sticks) softened unsalted butter, plus extra for greasing
175 g/6 oz (1¼ cups) self-raising flour
2 tablespoons desiccated (dried flaked) coconut
3 tablespoons plain yogurt, plus extra to serve (or you can use crème fraîche)
3 medium (US large) eggs
demerara (turbinado) sugar, for sprinkling

Preheat the oven to 180°C/350°F/Gas Mark 4 and grease and line a 20-cm/8-inch springform cake pan with baking (parchment) paper.

Put the gooseberries into a pan with the honey and a tablespoonful of water or the elderflower cordial (syrup), if using. Place over low heat and simmer until the gooseberries are just softened but still whole, about 5 minutes. Remove from the heat and let cool.

Beat the sugar and butter together in a large bowl until pale and fluffy. Add the flour, coconut, yogurt and eggs and mix until combined.

Tip the gooseberries into a sieve set over a bowl to collect the juices, reserving the syrupy juices for serving.

Gently fold the fruit into the batter mixture. Spoon the batter mixture into the prepared pan and sprinkle the top with demerara (turbinado) sugar.

Bake for 35 minutes, or until golden brown and a skewer inserted into the middle comes out clean. (This is a moist cake, so take care not to overcook it.) Let cool in the pan before removing and cutting into slices. Serve with yogurt or crème fraîche and a little of the reserved syrup.

SCENTED-LEAF PELARGONIUM SORBET

Serves 6–8

This sorbet is delicate and beautiful – the perfect light, refreshing dessert for a summer lunch in the garden. I use a variety of pelargonium called 'Attar of Roses' for this recipe, as it has the best and most characteristic rose geranium fragrance. Of all the plants I grow, I think this may be one of the ones that brings me most joy. It is beautiful to look at and scents the air when you brush against it. It is well worth growing, whether you plan to cook with it or not, but I do recommend that you try. I like to serve this sorbet with shortbread biscuits (cookies) flavoured with a little rosemary. The rich buttery biscuits are perfect alongside the cool fresh sorbet, and the flavour of herbs and flowers together is magical.

PREPARATION: 15 minutes,
   plus freezing

20 scented-leaf pelargonium leaves
200 g/7 oz (1 cup) caster
   (superfine) sugar
120 ml/4 fl oz (½ cup) lemon juice
   (about 3 large lemons)
shortbread (ideally, home-made
   shortbread flavoured with
   ½ teaspoon finely chopped
   rosemary), to serve

Put the pelargonium leaves into a food processor with the sugar and process until the mixture looks like a green paste. Add the lemon juice and process for another 15 seconds. Pour in 750 ml/1¼ pints (3 cups) cold water, process again, then strain the mixture through a very fine-mesh sieve set over a bowl to remove all the bits of leaf.

Pour the mixture into a lidded freezer-proof container and pop it into the freezer. When the mixture is firm but not rock-solid (about 2–3 hours), scrape the mixture into a food processor and process until smooth. Scoop the mixture back into the container and freeze once more. Repeat this process 2–3 times until the ice crystals are small and your sorbet mixture is smooth.

Remove the sorbet from the freezer about 30 minutes before you want to serve it, to soften it slightly (but this timing will all depend on the weather and the temperature in the room, so keep an eye on the sorbet). Serve scooped into bowls or dessert glasses with the shortbread biscuits (cookies).

Cakes & Desserts

FIG LEAF ICE-CREAM

Serves 6–8

The great thing about this recipe is that it makes use of the fig tree's extraordinary leaves. So even if you don't get enough sun to ripen the fruit, you can still enjoy the unique flavour of this wonderful plant, somehow sweet and green at the same time. Toasting the leaves makes a huge difference to the depth of flavour in the finished ice-cream.

PREPARATION: 15 minutes,
    plus infusing (steeping),
    chilling and freezing
COOKING: 15 minutes

4 fig leaves, washed and dried
475 ml/16 fl oz (2 cups) double (heavy) cream
475 ml/16 fl oz (2 cups) milk
200 g/7 oz (1 cup) caster (superfine) sugar
8 egg yolks
1 whole egg
pinch of salt
30 g/1¼ oz (scant ½ cup) (instant dry) whole milk powder

Toast the fig leaves over a gas flame until they are wilted and caramel coloured around the edges, but don't let them burn. Set aside to cool, then tear them into small pieces.

Heat the cream and milk with half the sugar in a heavy pan set over medium heat. Once the cream begins to boil, stir in the torn fig leaves, remove the pan from the heat and set aside to infuse (steep) for 15 minutes.

In a bowl, combine the egg yolks, whole egg, salt, (instant dry) milk powder and the remaining sugar and briskly whisk for 1 minute. Fill a large bowl with water and ice cubes.

Return the pan with the cream to the heat and bring it back up to a simmer, then strain the cream through a fine-mesh sieve into a jug (pitcher). Using a ladle, slowly pour some of the hot cream into the egg yolk mixture to warm it and loosen it slightly. Gradually pour the warmed egg mixture into the remaining hot cream in the pan, whisking constantly as you pour. Cook the custard over medium heat, stirring continuously and scraping the bottom of the pan with a rubber spatula or wooden spoon, until the custard thickens enough to coat the back of a spoon. Remove from the heat and place the pan of custard into the prepared bowl of iced water to cool completely, stirring it periodically and being careful not to get any splashes of water in the custard. Transfer the custard to a bowl and chill in the refrigerator for at least 2 hours, or overnight if you can.

Pour the custard into an ice-cream maker and churn according to the machine's directions. The ice-cream is ready once it has increased in volume, holds the lines from the stirring mechanism and mounds like softly whipped cream. Transfer the ice-cream to a lidded freezer-proof container and freeze for a few hours until firm before serving.

Cakes & Desserts

CHOCOLATE MOUSSE WITH ORANGE SALAD

Serves 8

This recipe comes from my friend Clare Birdsall's mother, Jeannie Jasper. Jeannie lived in Jerusalem for a while, where she cooked at a guesthouse called The American Colony. Then, it was a family-run affair, well known for its excellent food. Today it is a very glamorous hotel. This mousse is best made in advance – the flavour will improve with a little time spent resting in the refrigerator and, of course, that frees you up to relax and enjoy being with your guests. It is extremely rich, and a little goes a long way. I like to serve it with an orange salad, to freshen things up a little.

PREPARATION: 20 minutes,
  plus chilling
COOKING: 5 minutes

175 g/6 oz dark (semisweet)
  chocolate (ideally 72% cocoa
  solids), plus 1 tablespoon grated
  chocolate for decoration
6 eggs, separated
1 teaspoon dark rum
3 tablespoons caster (superfine)
  sugar
175 ml/6 fl oz (¾ cup) whipping
  cream
8 edible flowers (I like to use
  violas), to decorate

FOR THE ORANGE SALAD
4 ripe oranges
icing (confectioners') sugar, to taste
Grand Marnier or orange flower
  water (optional)

Melt the chocolate in a large heatproof bowl set over a pan of simmering water, making sure the bottom of the bowl does not touch the water. Remove it from the heat and let cool.

Using a fork, lightly beat the egg yolks together with the rum in a bowl. Stir them into the melted chocolate.

Beat the egg whites in a large bowl until thick and moussey, then whisk in the sugar, 1 teaspoon at a time, until soft peaks form. Set aside.

In another large bowl, whip the cream until soft peaks form. Fold the cream into the chocolate mixture, then fold in one-third of the egg whites to loosen the mixture slightly. Gently fold in the remainder of the egg whites so that the mousse is well blended. Divide the mousse between 8 small dessert dishes and chill in the refrigerator.

For the orange salad, slice off the peel and pith, standing each orange on a plate or shallow bowl as you do it to catch the juice. Cut the oranges into slices, arrange the slices on a plate and pour over the juice. Add a tiny sprinkle of icing (confectioners') sugar – the amount will depend on the sweetness of the oranges, and of your tooth. I like to drizzle over a little Grand Marnier, but you can also use orange flower water, if desired.

Sprinkle each mousse with a little grated chocolate, place an edible flower on top and serve with the orange salad.

BAKED APRICOTS WITH BAY AND HONEY

Serves 4–6

My friend Louise gave me this recipe. While there is very little better than a fresh apricot eaten straight from the tree, if you are lucky enough to have a good crop you will need to be a little more imaginative. Baking apricots is a great idea as it intensifies the flavour and will bring the best out of any fruit that is not quite perfectly ripe. The combination of spices in this syrup really does seem to bring out different aspects of the apricot's flavour – herbal and even a little spicy. Baking them whole, with the stones (pits) still inside, adds another layer of complexity, with nutty, almond flavours emerging. Try this alongside a scoop of good-quality vanilla ice-cream or with double (heavy) cream. (Of course, there is nothing to stop you having both.) This recipe would also work well with fresh peaches.

PREPARATION: 15 minutes
COOKING: 45 minutes

100 g/3½ oz (scant ⅓ cup) runny
   honey
5 cardamom pods, cracked opened
generous pinch of saffron threads
1 teaspoon coarse (kosher) sea salt
3 small bay leaves
10 apricots

Preheat the oven to 180°C/350°F/Gas Mark 4.

Put the honey, 100 ml/3½ fl oz (scant ½ cup) water, the cardamom pods, saffron, salt and bay leaves into a small pan. Place over medium heat and cook until the mixture comes to a boil. Simmer gently for 3 minutes and then remove from the heat.

Place the whole apricots in a small baking dish big enough to hold the apricots quite snugly – you don't want too much space between them. Pour over the honey mixture, using a wooden spoon or rubber spatula to scrape out any saffron threads that have stuck to the side of the pan.

Roast the apricots in the oven for 40 minutes, removing them to baste and turn every so often, or until they are very soft, but still hold their shape.

Remove from the heat and either serve immediately or set aside until cool and then store in the refrigerator until ready to serve.

BAKED CUSTARD WITH BLUEBERRIES

Serves 6

Cooking the blueberries in their own juices really helps to bring out their flavour and creates a wonderful contrast with the smooth, rich custard in this dessert. With blueberries, you will probably not need to use any additional sugar unless you have a very sweet tooth. If you decide to use fresh currants (black or red) instead, you may need a sprinkle. Figs, apricots and peaches will all work beautifully too.

PREPARATION: 15 minutes,
   plus infusing (steeping)
   and cooling
COOKING: 50–55 minutes

400 ml/14 fl oz (1⅔ cups) double
   (heavy) cream
200 ml/7 fl oz (scant 1 cup) milk
1 vanilla bean
10 egg yolks
65 g/2½ oz (⅓ cup) caster
   (superfine) sugar
350 g/12 oz (2½ cups) blueberries
2 teaspoons lemon or orange juice
   (or you could use water)

Preheat the oven to 140°C/275°F/Gas Mark 1.

Put the cream and milk into a pan. Split the vanilla bean down the middle and scrape the seeds into the pan – drop the bean in too. Stir well, then place over medium heat until it is just coming up to boiling point. Remove from the heat and let infuse (steep) for 40 minutes.

Beat the egg yolks and sugar together in a bowl until creamy and noticeably lighter in colour. Remove the vanilla bean from the cooled cream mixture before pouring it into the egg yolk and sugar mixture. Stir well to thoroughly combine.

Strain the mixture through a fine-mesh sieve into a shallow 23-cm/9-inch ovenproof dish and put into the oven. Bake for 35 minutes, then check to see if the custard is set; if not, give it another 5 minutes before checking again. It should be lightly golden on top and with a slight wobble in the centre – it will continue to firm up as it cools. Remove the custard from the oven and let cool.

Meanwhile, increase the oven temperature to 230°C/450°F/ Gas Mark 8. Put the blueberries into a separate shallow ovenproof dish and roast in the oven for 8 minutes, shaking the dish once during cooking to ensure that they are cooking evenly. You want them to be tender but not completely collapsed. Remove from the oven, immediately sprinkle with the fruit juice or water and shake the dish until some juices begin to form. Spoon over the baked custard before serving.

BAKED APPLES

Serves 3

When I was a child my father would often cook this dish in the winter. Now I have started to do the same for our symposiums at Great Dixter in the autumn and winter, when the cooking apples here in the UK are at their best. My friend and colleague Perry Rodriguez has come to love these baked apples nearly as much as I do. The great thing is that this recipe is so easy to scale up and cook for a crowd. I love the mix of tart apple flesh and sweet spices, along with the deep caramelized flavour of the maple syrup.

PREPARATION: 20 minutes
COOKING: 40 minutes

75 g/3 oz (⅓ cup packed) soft dark brown sugar
1½ teaspoons ground cinnamon
1½ teaspoons ground mixed (apple pie) spice
1½ teaspoons grated nutmeg
3 tablespoons maple syrup
75 g/3 oz (½ cup) raisins
3 large Bramley or other cooking apples (about 400 g/14 oz each)
40 g/1½ oz (3 tablespoons) butter

Preheat the oven to 180°C/350°F/Gas Mark 4.

Combine the sugar, spices, maple syrup and raisins in a bowl.

Core the apples and then open up the cavities a little more with the corer until they are about 2.5 cm/1 inch across. Take a thin slice off the bottom of the apples if necessary so that they sit flat, then make a very shallow cut around each apple to prevent them bursting during cooking.

Place the apples side-by-side in a shallow ovenproof dish. Pack the cavities with the sugar and spice mixture and put a tablespoon of butter on top of each apple.

Bake in the oven for 40 minutes, or until the sugar mixture is caramelized and the apples are tender through to the centre when pierced with a skewer. Let rest for 10 minutes before serving (the apples will be piping hot).

Cakes & Desserts

RHUBARB, ALMOND AND GINGER TART

Serves 8

Michael Morphy, the nursery manager at Great Dixter, has a great passion for the good things in life, and food is high on his list. I love doing weekend nursery duty with Michael as it is a great opportunity to talk about what we have been cooking and eating and to exchange recipes. When I heard him talk about this tart, I knew I had to include it in the book. It was the marzipan layer that sealed the deal – it is one of my passions.

First, make the rhubarb jam. Put the rhubarb into a pan with the sugar and stem (preserved) ginger and cook, covered, over low heat until the juices start to run from the fruit. Uncover and continue to simmer for 15–20 minutes, stirring regularly, until the excess liquid has disappeared and it has a thick, jam-like consistency. Set aside to cool completely.

Next, make the pastry (pie dough). Put the flour, ground almonds (almond meal), icing (confectioners') sugar and butter into a bowl and then, using your fingertips, rub in the butter until the mixture resembles fine breadcrumbs. Add the beaten egg and mix very briefly until a dough has formed. Shape into a ball, cover with clingfilm (plastic wrap) and chill in the refrigerator for 20–30 minutes.

Grease a 27-cm/10½-inch loose-bottom tart pan with butter. Roll out the pastry on a lightly floured work counter until it is large enough to line the bottom and sides of the tart pan. Let rest in the refrigerator for 20 minutes while you preheat the oven to 200°C/400°F/Gas Mark 6. Slide a baking sheet into the oven.

Meanwhile, put the blanched almonds in a bowl, cover with boiling water and let soak for 10 minutes. Drain and dry well, then cut lengthwise into thin slivers. Sprinkle over a baking sheet and toast in the oven for about 8 minutes until lightly golden. (You can also use the same amount of flaked/slivered almonds, toasted quickly in the oven or in a dry frying pan or skillet.)

PREPARATION: 20 minutes,
    plus cooling and chilling
COOKING: 1¾ –2 hours

FOR THE RHUBARB JAM
450 g/1 lb forced rhubarb, cut into
    1-cm/½-inch pieces (3⅔ cups
    prepared)
2 tablespoons caster (superfine)
    sugar
100 g/3½ oz stem (preserved)
    ginger, coarsely chopped
    (⅓ cup prepared)

FOR THE PASTRY (PIE DOUGH)
200 g/7 oz (1⅔ cups) plain
    (all-purpose) flour, plus extra
    for dusting
60 g/2½ oz (⅔ cup) ground almonds
    (almond meal)
100 g/3½ oz (¾ cup plus 1 tablespoon)
    icing (confectioners') sugar
160 g/5½ oz (1¾ sticks) chilled
    unsalted butter, diced, plus extra
    for greasing
1 tablespoon beaten egg

FOR THE TOPPING AND FILLING
40 g/1½ oz (¼ cup) blanched almonds
180 g/6 oz (1½ sticks) unsalted butter,
    at room temperature, diced
180 g/6 oz (generous ¾ cup) golden
    caster (superfine) sugar
140 g/5 oz (1½ cups) ground almonds
    (almond meal)
40 g/1½ oz (⅓ cup) plain (all-
    purpose) flour
4 medium (US large) eggs, beaten
60 g/2½ oz stem (preserved) ginger,
    coarsely chopped (3½ tablespoons
    prepared)

Line the pastry case (shell) with a crumpled sheet of baking (parchment) paper and fill it with baking beans (pie weights). Place the pan on the hot baking sheet and bake for 20–25 minutes until the edges are a gentle gold colour. Remove from the oven, let cool slightly and then very carefully remove the paper and beans (take care as the pastry is very short). Protect the edges of the pastry case with narrow strips of aluminium foil and return to the oven for 5–7 minutes until the bottom is golden brown. Remove from the oven and let cool. Lower the oven temperature to 180°C/350°F/Gas Mark 4.

For the almond filling, cream the butter and sugar together in a bowl until pale and fluffy, then beat in the ground almonds, flour and eggs, one-third at a time. Fold in the stem ginger.

When the pastry case has cooled, spread the rhubarb jam over the bottom of the tart. Then gently spread the almond filling over the jam, sprinkle over the toasted almonds and bake for 45 minutes, or until golden and a skewer pushed into the centre of the tart comes out clean. If it looks like the tart is browning too quickly, cover with a loose sheet of aluminium foil towards the end of cooking. Serve warm or at room temperature.

BLACKCURRANT TART

Serves 8

Mrs Next Door is a great friend who generously allows me to use her beautiful greenhouse to get my seeds going in spring and overwinter some of my tender plants. This is an old family recipe of hers, and a very simple one, that makes great use of the tart flavour of blackcurrants.

PREPARATION: 15 minutes,
    plus chilling
COOKING: 40–45 minutes

350 g/12 oz (2¾ cups) plain
    (all-purpose) flour, plus extra
    for dusting
2 teaspoons ground cinnamon
350 g/12 oz (1¾ cups) caster
    (superfine) sugar, plus
    1 tablespoon, for sprinkling
150 g/5 oz (1¼ sticks) butter,
    softened
4 medium (US large) egg yolks
700 g/1 lb 8½ oz (6¼ cups)
    blackcurrants
1 egg white

Tip the flour onto a clean work counter. Sprinkle over the cinnamon, make a well in the centre and put 150 g/5 oz (¾ cup) of the sugar, the butter and egg yolks into the middle. Work the sugar, butter and egg yolks together with your fingertips, then gradually blend in the flour and cinnamon to form a smooth paste, adding a little cold water if necessary to help bring the pastry (pie dough) together. As soon as the mixture comes together, form the dough into a ball, cover with clingfilm (plastic wrap) and chill in the refrigerator for 30 minutes.

Meanwhile, put the currants into a pan over low heat with 200 g/7 oz (1 cup) of the remaining sugar and 2 teaspoons of cold water. Cook slowly at first to burst the skins, then turn up the heat so that the mixture bubbles and reduces down to a thick, rich-looking sauce. This should take no more than 8–10 minutes. Pour the mixture into a bowl and let cool.

Slide a baking sheet into the oven and preheat the oven to 200°C/400°F/Gas Mark 6.

Roll out half the pastry on a lightly floured work counter until it is large enough to line the bottom and sides of a 24-cm/9½-inch loose-bottom tart pan that is no more than 2 cm/¾ inch deep. Gather up the pastry trimmings (scraps), knead them with the remaining pastry and roll out into a disc that is slightly larger than the top of the pan. Cut it across into 1-cm/½-inch wide strips. Pour the currant mixture into the pastry case (shell) and arrange the pastry strips on top in a lattice pattern, pressing them well onto the edge of the pastry case. Brush the pastry strips with the egg white and sprinkle with a little of the extra sugar. Place the pan on the hot baking sheet and bake for 30–35 minutes until the pastry is crisp and nicely browned. Remove from the oven and sprinkle the top of the tart with the remaining extra sugar.

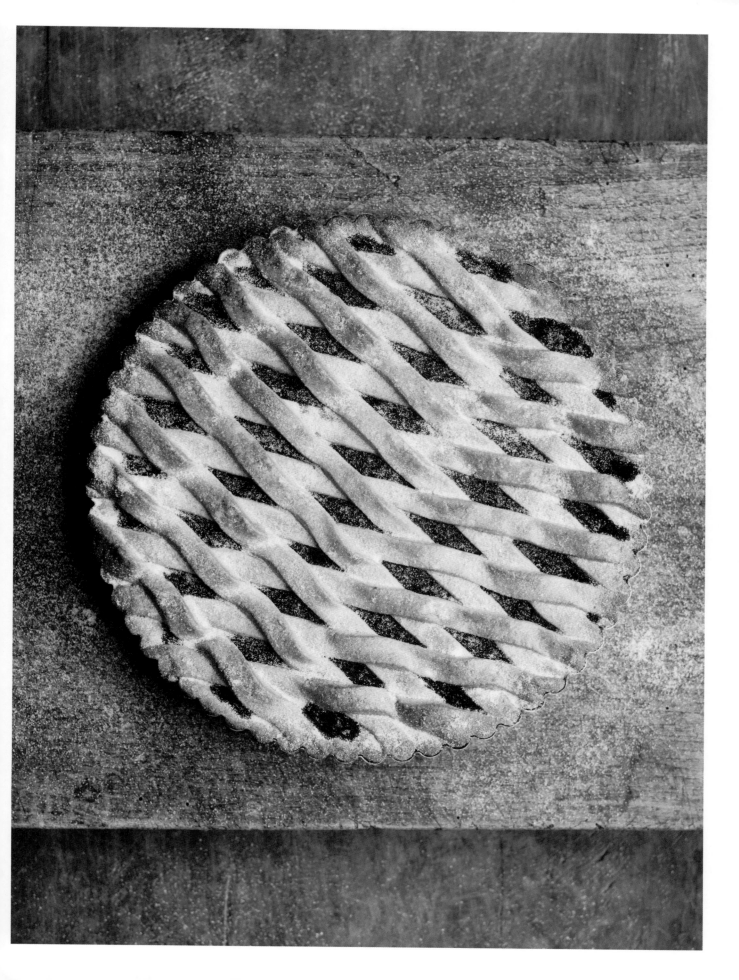

BASIL PAVLOVA

Serves 12

This pavlova recipe from my friend Isabelle Smith is a wonderful variation on the classic theme. Basil is a great partner for summer fruit and also turns the meringue the most delicate pale green.

PREPARATION: 20 minutes,
   plus cooling
COOKING: 1 hour

400 g/14 oz (2 cups) caster
   (superfine) sugar
25 g/1 oz (1 cup) basil leaves
7 egg whites
pinch of cream of tartar
2 teaspoons cornflour (cornstarch)
2 teaspoons white wine vinegar
300 g/11 oz (2⅔ cups) summer
   berries (use fresh currants,
   raspberries, Alpine strawberries
   or whatever you have to hand)
250 g/9 oz (1 cup) mascarpone
   cheese
300 ml/10½ fl oz (1¼ cups) double
   (heavy) cream
2 tablespoons Grand Marnier,
   or more, to taste
1 tablespoon icing (confectioners')
   sugar

Preheat the oven to 150°C/300°F/Gas Mark 2. Line 2 baking sheets with baking (parchment) paper and mark each one with a 20-cm/8-inch circle. Flip the paper over so that the pencil marks are on the underside.

Put the caster (superfine) sugar and basil into a food processor and process until the basil is reduced to fine specks and the sugar has turned light green.

In a large bowl, whisk the egg whites with the cream of tartar until soft peaks form. Add 350 g/12 oz (1¾ cups) of the basil sugar mixture to the egg whites, 1 tablespoon at a time, until the mixture is stiff and glossy. Whisk in the cornflour (cornstarch) and vinegar. Once all the sugar is incorporated, you should have a beautiful pale green meringue mixture.

Divide the mixture between the prepared baking sheets and spread out within the marked lines to form discs. Bake for 1 hour, or until the meringue is firm and slightly golden on top. Then, without opening the door, turn off the oven and let the pavlova cool inside.

Meanwhile, put the berries in a bowl and stir in the remaining 50 g/2 oz (¼ cup) of the basil sugar mixture. Let macerate while the pavlova is cooling in the oven.

Just before serving, put the mascarpone into a bowl and whisk briefly until softened. Add the cream, Grand Marnier and icing (confectioners') sugar and whisk together until soft peaks form.

Once the meringues are cooled, carefully lift them off the baking paper. Place 1 disc onto a serving plate and spoon over the mascarpone cream, swirling it out to the edges. Spoon over some of the berries and top with the second meringue disc. Top with the remaining berries.

SUMMER PUDDING

Serves 6–8

This recipe was given to me by Nell Jones, head gardener at London's Chelsea Physic Garden. If you have a bumper crop of fruit, double the quantity and stash half in the freezer.

Preheat the oven to 170°C/325°F/Gas Mark 3 and grease and line the bottoms of 2 deep 20-cm/8-inch round sandwich (cake) pans.

First, make the sponge cake. Sift the flour and baking powder into a bowl, add the remaining ingredients and use an electric hand whisk (handheld mixer) to mix everything together until well combined. Divide the batter between the prepared sandwich pans and bake for 20–25 minutes until the cakes are golden brown and just coming away from the edges of the pan. Turn out onto wire racks and let cool completely.

Put the gooseberries and currants into a pan with the sugar. Bring to a boil, then reduce the heat and simmer for about 10 minutes. Remove from the heat and add the remaining fruit, stirring carefully so that the fruit is evenly mixed. Tip the fruit into a sieve set over a bowl to collect the fruit juice.

Line a 1-litre/1¾-pint (4¼-cup) pudding basin (deep ovenproof dish) with clingfilm (plastic wrap), leaving plenty overhanging. Pour the fruit juice into a shallow dish. Take one of the sponge cakes and cut it across into slices about 1–1.5-cm/½ –¾-inch thick and then cut them to match the depth of your pudding basin. Dip the strips of sponge into the fruit juice and use to line the pudding basin, overlapping the slices slightly and making sure there are no gaps.

Spoon in the fruit and 3 tablespoons of the remaining fruit juice. Cut a round piece of cake from the second sponge, approximately 14 cm/5½ inches across, to fit snugly across the top of the basin. Press down firmly and then cover the surface of the sponge with the overhanging clingfilm and then a saucer or small plate. Put a weight on top and leave in the refrigerator for several hours, or overnight if possible.

Just before serving, fold back the clingfilm and invert the pudding onto a flat serving plate. Brush with the remaining fruit juice. Serve cut into wedges with crème fraîche.

PREPARATION: 10 minutes,
 plus cooling and chilling
COOKING: 30–35 minutes

FOR THE SPONGE
225 g/8 oz (1⅔ cups) self-raising
 flour
1 rounded teaspoon baking powder
4 medium (US large) eggs
225 g/8 oz (2 cups plus
 2 tablespoons) caster (superfine)
 sugar
225 g/8 oz (2 sticks) butter,
 at room temperature, plus extra
 for greasing
½ teaspoon vanilla extract

FOR THE PUDDING
100 g/3½ oz (⅔ cup) gooseberries,
 trimmed
100 g/3½ oz (scant 1 cup)
 blackcurrants, trimmed
150 g/5 oz (1⅓ cups) redcurrants,
 trimmed
75 g/3 oz (⅓ cup) caster (superfine)
 sugar
250 g/9 oz (2 cups) raspberries
150 g/5 oz (1 cup) strawberries,
 hulled and cut into pieces the
 same size as your raspberries
crème fraîche, to serve

PEACH COBBLER

Serves 6

My friend Linda Smith is a true Southern girl and her cooking style reflects this. This cobbler reminds me of staying with her on her farm outside Memphis, where she grows the most wonderful fruit. The great thing about this dish is that you can enjoy it at all times of the year, using whatever fruit is in season – or stashed away in your freezer. I'm thinking apricots, apples, figs, blueberries, raspberries … really, the possibilities are endless. It is also very quick and easy to make, so perfect for unexpected guests. I like to serve it warm, with plenty of double (heavy) cream.

PREPARATION: 10 minutes
COOKING: 40–45 minutes

3 large ripe peaches
50 g/2 oz (4 tablespoons) butter
160 g/5½ oz self-raising flour
¼ teaspoon fine salt
250 g/9 oz (1¼ cups) caster (superfine) sugar
240 ml/7¾ fl oz (1 cup) evaporated milk
double (heavy) cream, to serve

Preheat the oven to 180°C/350°F/Gas Mark 4. Halve the peaches, remove and discard the stones (pits) and cut the fruit into wedges.

Put the butter into a 23 x 33-cm/9 x 13-inch shallow ovenproof dish, place it in the oven and let the butter melt.

Meanwhile, sift the flour and salt into a bowl and stir in 200 g/7 oz (1 cup) of the sugar. Make a well in the centre, add the evaporated milk and gradually whisk together to make a smooth batter.

Take the dish out of the oven and pour the batter evenly over the bottom of the dish. Arrange the peach slices on top and sprinkle with 1 tablespoon of the sugar. Bake for 40-45 minutes until the peaches are cooked through and the batter is puffed up and golden and crisp at the edges. The batter will rise and the fruit will sink. Remove from the oven, sprinkle with the remaining sugar and serve hot with cream.

PRESERVES & DRINKS

JO'S PESTO

PRESERVED LEMONS

EASY PICKLED VEGETABLES

BASIL JELLY

JAYNE'S BEST-IN-THE-WORLD DREAMY MOJITO

RHUBARB GIN

FRUIT VODKA

JO'S PESTO

Makes 1 x 400-ml/14-fl oz (US 12-fl oz) jar

It is not every day you meet someone who simultaneously makes you want to sit down and talk to them for hours, and also leap on the first train home, run to the vegetable garden and start making dinner. Jo, whom I met at the Barbican performing arts centre in London, is just such a person. She grows vegetables with such passion and energy, despite the limited space at her disposal. This pesto is completely seasonal. Make it using whatever leafy greens you have, at any time of year. You can even use beetroot tops (beet greens) too. The only rule is to make sure the leaves are as young and tender as possible – otherwise you will be chewing for days.

PREPARATION: 10 minutes

80 g/3 oz (2–3 cups) green leaves, such as soft herbs, sorrel and Swiss chard in the summer; rocket (arugula), kale, parsley and Asian greens in the winter
50 g/2 oz (⅓ cup) pumpkin seeds
3 cloves garlic, very finely chopped
40 g/1½ oz (½ cup) grated Parmesan cheese
120 ml/4 fl oz (½ cup) extra virgin olive oil
salt and pepper

Place the leaves (greens) and pumpkin seeds into the bowl of a food processor and pulse a few times until coarsely chopped. Add the garlic and Parmesan and pulse a few more times. Scrape down the sides of the food processor with a rubber spatula.

Add the olive oil slowly, while the processor is running, occasionally stopping it to scrape down the sides with the spatula. Stop when everything is evenly amalgamated and you have a thick, glossy, vibrant green sauce. Season to taste with salt and pepper.

Spoon into a warm, sterilized glass jar (see page 234), pour a little more oil over the top and seal immediately. Store in the refrigerator for up to 3 weeks (or freeze in ice-cube trays).

PRESERVED LEMONS

Makes 1 x 1-litre/1¾-pint (US 32-fl oz) Kilner jar

I have used 'lemons' in the plural for the title of this recipe but if your lemon tree gives you only a single fruit, I still urge you to follow this recipe. Even just one preserved lemon in a jar in the refrigerator will add so much to so many dishes: salad dressings, tagines, pilafs, roasted vegetables, there is little that isn't enhanced with the addition of some of the finely chopped, intensely citrusy salty flesh and zest. There are a million ways to make preserved lemons, but this is how I do it.

PREPARATION: 10 minutes,
    plus infusing (steeping)

6 small unwaxed lemons
approx. 100 g/3½ oz (scant ½ cup)
    fine crystal sea salt
2 bay leaves
5–6 cloves

Sterilize a jar (see page 234) that is large enough to accommodate your lemons – remember you will be squishing them down quite hard to release as much juice as possible.

Wash the lemons, stand them upright and then, cutting downwards, make 4 lengthwise slits in each lemon, making sure not to cut all the way through the bottom.

Sprinkle a thin layer of salt in the bottom of the jar. Sprinkle some salt into each lemon, allowing about 1 teaspoon of salt for each fruit, and pushing it well down into the cracks. Push each lemon down into the jar, using a decent amount of pressure so that the juice starts to flow. Add the bay leaves and cloves, top the jar up with boiling water and then seal immediately. Let cool, then keep at room temperature for a couple of days, shaking the jar every so often, before storing in the refrigerator. The preserved lemons will last for a good 2–3 months; the longer you can leave them before using them, the more intense the flavour will be.

EASY PICKLED VEGETABLES

Fills 4 x 1-litre/1¾-pint (US 32-fl oz) Kilner jars

My friend Dr Kyle is the person who supplies me with the seeds I need each year for the garden. She is also a great cook, so I was delighted when she shared this recipe with me. I love to stay with her and have her cook for me, as she always makes a dessert I love, chocolate angel pie. Slightly less extravagant but possibly more useful are these easy pickles. Kyle uses beetroot (beets), but you can use carrots or radishes as well. Cucumbers will work too, although they should not be boiled before adding the pickling liquid. Keep any extras in a non-reactive container in a cool place. I love to eat these pickles with a dollop of yogurt or sour cream as a salad or side dish – great with leftover meat, or added to a salad.

Put the beetroot (beets), carrots and radishes into separate pans of boiling water and cook until they are only just soft to the point of a knife. Drain and set aside to cool.

When the beetroot is cool enough to handle, rub off and discard the beetroot skin. (This is a bloody business, so I advise you to wear rubber gloves.)

Make the pickling liquid. Put the sugar, vinegar and 750 ml/ 1¼ pints (3 cups) of water into a pan. Slowly bring to a boil, stirring now and then to dissolve the sugar, then remove from the heat, add the cloves and let cool slightly.

Pack the beetroot, carrots, radishes and cucumbers into individual warm, sterilized Kilner jars (see page 234), top with the sliced onions and pour in enough pickling liquid to cover the vegetables generously. Seal immediately and leave for at least 24 hours so the flavours can come together. Store in the refrigerator or a cool, dark place. The pickles will last for a good 2–3 months.

PREPARATION: 20 minutes, plus cooling and infusing (steeping)
COOKING: 20 minutes

1 kg/2¼ lb small raw beetroot (beets), trimmed
350 g/12 oz baby carrots, trimmed
500 g/1 lb 2 oz radishes, trimmed
2 small ridge-style cucumbers, halved and cut lengthwise into wedges
2 large sweet white onions (look for ones sold as salad or Spanish onions, otherwise the flavour will be overpowering), halved and thinly sliced

FOR THE PICKLING LIQUID
750 g/1 lb 10 oz (3¾ cups) caster (superfine) sugar
750 ml/1¼ pints (3 cups) raw (apple) cider vinegar
5 cloves

Preserves & Drinks

BASIL JELLY

Makes 5 x 200-ml/7-fl oz (US 8-fl oz) jars

This recipe is another from Dr Kyle's kitchen. If you are using green basil, you may want to add a drop or two of green food colouring to make the colour a little stronger. If you use purple basil, the jelly will be a very pretty pale amethyst. This is wonderful served alongside roast lamb or chicken.

Place a saucer in the refrigerator.

Put the basil into a pan and pour over 400 ml/14 fl oz (1⅔ cups) boiling water, mashing the leaves thoroughly to make sure you are extracting maximum flavour – just as you would if you were making herbal tea. Let cool.

Set the pan of 'tea' over medium-high heat, add the lemon juice and sugar and stir until the sugar has melted. Bring to a boil, add the liquid pectin and continue to boil for a full minute. Test to see if the jelly has set by placing a teaspoonful of the hot mixture onto the chilled saucer and run the end of a wooden spoon through it – if a line stays, it is done; if not, boil a little longer, then test again. When ready, remove from the heat, skim off any froth from the surface and pour through a very fine-mesh sieve into a jug (pitcher) and then pour into warm, sterilized jars (see page 234) and seal immediately. Label and date, then store in a cool, dry place. Once opened, keep in the refrigerator.

PREPARATION: 10 minutes,
  plus cooling
COOKING: 30 minutes

75 g/3 oz (2½ cups) basil leaves,
  finely chopped
juice of 1 lemon
700 g/1 lb 8½ oz (3½ cups) caster
  (superfine) sugar
75 ml/3 fl oz (1 pouch) liquid pectin
  – I use Certo (alternatively, you
  can use 1 x 8-g sachet/1 x 1¼-oz
  US box powdered pectin, stirring
  it into the sugar before you start
  to make the jelly)

Preserves & Drinks

JAYNE'S BEST-IN-THE-WORLD DREAMY MOJITO

Serves 1

The name of this recipe tells you all you need to know. Jayne Gillespie is a great gardening friend and diligent about making sure you do not dry out when you are working with her. Strangely, we seem to get more done in the morning than we do after lunch. The directions in the recipe are Jayne's, and clearly make the point that just as with all cooking, when making a cocktail it is worth taking care at every step and using the best ingredients you can. The shot measure is used here to give you the proportions, but you can easily scale this up for a party by using a larger glass as your measure. You will need a cocktail shaker.

PREPARATION: 5 minutes

½ lime (or ¾ shot shop-bought lime juice)
handful mint leaves
1 shot three-year-old Havana rum (don't be tempted to try this with an inferior rum – it won't be the same)
¾ shot sugar syrup (I use Monin's pure cane sugar syrup or make my own)
crushed ice, to serve

Cut the lime half into 4 pieces and put into a cocktail shaker with the mint.

Using the end of a wooden rolling pin, bash the lime segments (sections) and mint leaves to bruise and release the delicious mint, lime zest and juice (this is important as the lime juice is needed to balance the sugar syrup). Next, add the rum and sugar syrup. Shake well and then pour into a glass filled with crushed ice.

Alternatively, you can mix the cocktail in a jug (pitcher), let chill in the refrigerator and then add the crushed ice just before serving.

RHUBARB GIN

Makes 500 ml/18 fl oz (generous 2 cups)

What to say about rhubarb gin? It is the nectar of the gods. This recipe is the result of a treadmill brainstorming session with Mrs Next Door. During our gym sessions we often talk about food and drink. A little ironic, I suppose, but what is the point of burning off all those calories if you're not going to take a few more on? She was telling me about a cocktail she'd had, made with rhubarb gin. It sounded delicious, so I thought I would try it. I never got as far as making the cocktail – the gin was just too delicious on its own. The trick is to keep the sugar levels low, using just enough to bring out the flavour of the rhubarb. This makes an amazing digestif, as it is so refreshing.

PREPARATION: 15 minutes, plus infusing (steeping)

400 g/14 oz rhubarb (about 8 stalks), trimmed and cut into 5-cm/2-inch pieces
4 tablespoons caster (superfine) sugar, or to taste
500 ml/18 fl oz (generous 2 cups) gin

Place the fruit in a warm, sterilized Kilner jar (see page 234), then add the sugar, followed by the gin. Seal the jar and shake well. Let infuse (steep) for 4 days or so in a cool, dark place, giving it a good shake every day. Taste and add more sugar, if desired.

Strain through a muslin (cheesecloth)-lined funnel into warm, sterilized bottles, reserving the infused rhubarb pieces to use to make a fool, or freeze them for another time.

Serve the gin really, really cold. It will keep for months – if you don't drink it all at once!

FRUIT VODKA

Tom Coward's flavoured vodka is the best I've ever tasted, because the flavour of the fruit is front and centre. Traditional recipes work by volume – one-third alcohol, one-third fruit and one-third sugar. Tom's does the same, the difference being that you don't add the sugar until later, giving you the chance to taste as you add and stop at the point where the balance is just right for that particular fruit. This is a brilliant recipe to try if you only have a small amount of fruit to play with. You could even make it in a jam jar. Once the vodka is ready, strain it, decant into bottles and keep it in the freezer.

PREPARATION: 15 minutes,
    plus infusing (steeping)

fruit, such as forced rhubarb, fresh
    currants, Alpine strawberries or
    raspberries
decent-quality vodka – the better
    the quality, the better the results
caster (superfine) sugar, to taste

Wash and pick over, trim or chop the fruit as needed (you can leave currants, Alpine strawberries and raspberries whole).

Place the fruit in a warm, sterilized Kilner jar or bottle (see page 234), then pour over vodka until you have equal 'layers' of fruit and vodka. Let infuse (steep) for as long as it takes for the fruit flavour to seep out into the vodka – at least a week. When you are happy that the vodka is fruity enough, add sugar, a little a time, shaking or stirring to dissolve, and tasting every now and again. Stop adding sugar when you're happy with the balance.

Let infuse for 1 month, up-ending the jar or bottle every now and again, to make sure that the sugar is fully dissolved and the flavours melded. Strain through a muslin (cheesecloth)-lined funnel into warm, sterilized bottles, reserving the infused fruit to use to make a fool, or freeze them for another time.

Serve the vodka really, really cold – I like to store it in the freezer. It will keep for months.

Preserves & Drinks

GLOSSARY

Annual – An annual is any plant that completes its life cycle – from germination through to setting seed and dying – within a single year. The majority of vegetables are annual plants.

Blight – A fungal disease that affects first foliage, then fruit and tubers. In the UK we see it most often in late summer on potatoes and tomatoes. As soon as you see the foliage start to turn brown, you must act to remove the blighted parts of the plants immediately and put them on a bonfire. If burning them is not an option, they will just have to be thrown away. Whatever you do, don't add them to your garden compost; the spores will survive and potentially infect your plants the following year.

Blood, fish and bone meal – A slow-release fertilizer that should be added to the soil in spring, just as plants are starting to put on growth. The mixture contains nitrogen, phosphorus and potassium – all the nutrients needed for healthy leaves, fruit and roots – and also improves soil health by supporting bacteria and beneficial fungi in the soil. It is worth noting that many dogs – my own included – consider the fertilizer a great delicacy, so fork it well into the soil and water in if it does not rain soon afterwards.

Bolting – When a plant bolts it is simply fulfilling its natural urge to reproduce by producing flowers and seeds. Unfortunately for us it also means that the crops become tough, bitter and eventually inedible. To an extent it is unavoidable – but regular picking and conscientious watering will extend the plant's useful life for as long as possible.

Companion planting – Planting two or more different plants close to each other in order to achieve a particular effect, most commonly as a natural form of pest control or to promote pollination. For example, planting chives next to carrots will deter carrot fly, while herbs and edible flowers such as nasturtiums will attract pollinators to your patch.

Cordon tree – These consist of a single vertical main stem, with the fruit carried on very short lateral branches. This is an excellent and very efficient way of growing fruit in a small area. A cordon tree will need to be supported with a strong stake, or tied into a trellis or other framework against a wall.

Cotyledon – An embryonic leaf. When a seed starts to germinate, it first puts down a root to anchor the plant and feed it. Next, it puts up a stem with two cotyledons, also known as seed leaves, in order to start the process of photosynthesis. Rounded in shape, the cotyledons of most plants look quite similar. The 'true' leaves are next to emerge, and these will look like the leaves of the mature plant.

Damping-off – This occurs when pathogens weaken or kill a seed or seedling. It is most likely to occur when the soil or compost (potting soil) is too wet or cold, and there is poor air circulation. Telltale signs include discolouration and shrinkage around the base of the seedlings, or a failure to germinate.

Dwarfing rootstock – Most commercially available fruit trees consist of two parts, grafted together. The top part produces the fruit, while the bottom part – or rootstock – will dictate the eventual size of the tree (although the size of the fruit itself will always be the same). When selecting fruit trees to grow in containers, choose trees grown on dwarfing rootstocks. Look for words such as 'dwarf', 'patio' and 'container' on the labels, or the codes 'M9' (for dwarfing) or 'M27' (for very dwarfing).

Ericaceous compost – This compost is specially formulated for acid-loving plants, such as blueberries. In ordinary compost acid-loving plants will struggle to access the nutrients they need for healthy growth.

Espalier – This method of training fruit trees is very useful for creating a boundary or when you need to plant a tree against a wall or fence. Espaliered trees grow flat, and consist of a central leader with symmetrical branches leading out from it. These branches will need to be tied to a sturdy frame. Espaliered trees should be pruned twice a year: once in winter, to get rid of any old or diseased wood and maintain the shape of the tree; and then again in mid-summer to take out the floppy new growth and keep it looking neat.

Fan training – A method of training fruit trees – as the name suggests – into the shape of an open fan, with symmetrical branches emerging at an angle from the central stem. As with other methods of training, this is an excellent and very efficient way of growing fruit in a confined space. Fan-trained trees will need a good strong support.

Fleece and crop covers – Protective coverings used to help warm the soil, and protect young plants from frost and pests. The most common type is horticultural fleece, a lightweight fabric made from polypropylene. I use this at the start of the season to cover areas where seed has been sown or seedlings planted out. It is permeable, so water can get through.

Forcing – Generally in gardening our aim is to ensure that plants get as much light as possible. With forcing, we do exactly the opposite in order to force the plants into early growth. The general principle is to wait until the plant – most commonly rhubarb, chicory (Belgian endive) or sea kale – starts into growth, then cover it completely. Starved of light, the new shoots will grow tender and free of fibres, although the process will significantly weaken the plant.

Germination – The point at which a seed begins to turn into a new plant, first putting down roots and then sprouting a set of cotyledons – or seed leaves. Germination requires a combination of warmth, light and moisture.

Horticultural grit – Washed grit, with each piece having a diameter of up to about 5 mm (¼ inch), is invaluable in the container garden for ensuring good drainage. I add about one part grit to nine parts compost (potting soil) when potting up plants such as rosemary, thyme and scented-leaf pelargoniums, which will rot if left to sit in a too-wet soil.

Interplanting – This describes the practice of growing more than one crop together, most often something quick to harvest – such as radishes or salad leaves (greens) – with something slower to mature. It could also mean combining crops with different habits – a climbing bean, say, with creeping thyme. The idea is to make the best use of the available space.

Maiden – A maiden is a one-year-old fruit tree. They are sold in two different forms: a maiden whip consists of the central stem only while a feathered maiden will also have some side branches. This is by far the cheapest way of buying fruit trees, and gives you the flexibility to train the tree into any shape you like, but you will need to wait a couple of years for your fruit.

Mulch – A layer of material used to cover the ground in order to suppress weeds and retain moisture. At Great Dixter we use organic material as it also helps to improve the soil around the roots of the plants. Other types of mulch include bark chips, gravel, shredded newspaper and straw.

Perennial – Any plant that lives longer than two years can be described as perennial, but the word is mainly applied to herbaceous plants as opposed to those with woody stems. Typically, a perennial will put up new growth in the spring, fruit or flower in summer, then die back in autumn/winter. Perennial vegetable plants include sorrel and asparagus.

Plug plants – Seedlings that have been grown on in trays that consist of a number of small cells. Plug plants are widely available in nurseries and garden centres – or, of course, you can prick out your own seedlings into plug trays. The great thing about them is that they are the perfect size to be planted out into their final position. Push the plants up and out from the bottom of the cell, keeping the soil around the roots intact as far as possible.

Pollination – The transfer of pollen from the male part of a plant (the anther) to the female (stigma), triggering fertilization and the production of flowers, fruit and ultimately seeds. Sometimes this involves two separate plants, but in some cases pollination can also occur within the same plant. Such plants are known as self-fertile.

Powdery mildew – A common fungal disease that looks like grey powder. It appears on the leaves and stems and will weaken and ultimately kill the plant. Good air circulation is the best way of preventing it. You can also make your own spray to control powdery mildew by combining bicarbonate of soda (baking soda) with water and a little vegetable oil.

Rust – A fungal disease that affects mainly the leaves of plants, such as leeks and broad (fava) beans, and also fruit trees. The pustules vary in colour, but are often orange or rusty looking. As rust weakens plants, opening them up to other diseases, you need to be vigilant and burn any affected as soon as you see the signs.

Self-pollinating – A plant that does not need another plant to pollinate its flowers. There are two types of self-pollinator: with the first, pollination takes place within a single flower; with the second, pollen is moved from one flower to another on the same plant.

Slips – This refers to the side shoots of an artichoke plant, cut away from the main plant. This is a very good way of rejuvenating your artichokes and keeping them cropping well. Each slip should have a good section of root and a strong growing point.

Succession sowing – This simply means sowing – and/or planting – little and often, rather than all at once. This will help to ensure continued availability of crops such as salads, which will quickly run to seed if not picked regularly, and also extend the season so that you can enjoy your produce for longer.

Top dressing This involves removing the top layer of compost in a container and replacing it with fresh compost to provide the plant with nutrients. You can also take the opportunity to add some fertilizer, such as blood, fish and bone. This is a great way of refreshing plants such as fruit trees that stay in their pots for several years at a stretch.

DEALING WITH PESTS

This is not intended to be a definitive guide to pest control. The pests you encounter will vary enormously, depending on location, climate and the types of crops you are growing, so it is worth sourcing a comprehensive and reliable source of information, whether in printed form or online.

Listed here are some of the most common pests and my favoured remedies. Note that while I am not strictly organic in my gardening, I do tend towards the minimal in my pest control. I am not concerned with growing perfect-looking crops. If they are slightly nibbled around the edges, so be it. More important to me is that they taste good and are as chemical-free as possible. When it comes to pests, early intervention is probably the best preventative, and is quite manageable with container gardening because the scale is small. It's easy to look at your pots every day and spot when things first start to go wrong.

APHIDS OR GREENFLY

Aphids tend to appear on new growth. They are sap-sucking insects, so will cause plants to grow distorted and weak, encouraging the transmission of viruses. They also deposit a sticky honeydew on plants, which attracts moulds. Being relatively large insects, aphids are easy to spot. Tackle them early by simply squashing them between your fingers. If the numbers start to increase, squirt plants with a weak solution of washing-up liquid (dish soap) in water – just add a few drops to a spray bottle. Growing nasturtiums (see page 107) and French marigolds (see page 109) will help too. Greenfly love these plants, and tend to flock to them in preference, leaving your precious crops alone.

BIRDS

While birds can be enormously helpful in keeping slugs and snails under control, they are fickle friends and will quickly switch preference at the first sign of your soft fruit becoming ripe. I use netting to keep them off (see page 50).

CAPSID BUG

Green or brown, and about 6 mm (¼ inch) long, some varieties of capsid bug are harmless. Others are sap-suckers that will distort the growth of your plants and pepper the leaves with holes. While these bugs will attack crops such as climbing beans and potatoes, they seem to prefer fruit bushes and trees – look out for patchy skin on young fruit. As far as I am aware, there is no organic remedy, and since the patchiness does not affect the taste of the fruit, I am inclined to live with it and simply pinch off any particularly damaged leaves. You can reduce the bugs' chances of surviving the winter and returning next year by pruning out dead or damaged growth, staying on top of the weeding and keeping the area tidy and free of plant debris.

FLEA BEETLE

If you've ever been driven mad by hundreds of small holes appearing in your otherwise healthy-looking salad leaves (greens), meet the culprit. Flea beetles – tiny, dark and flat – seem to be particularly fond of peppery crops, such as rocket (arugula), mizuna and mustards. I find the best way to control them is to sow late, from mid-summer onwards, when they are less active. This has the added benefit of making your crops less likely to bolt and run to seed too quickly. Covering young crops with horticultural fleece is very effective too (see page 50).

SLUGS AND SNAILS

Quite possibly enemy number one for those of us gardening in a damp, temperate climate, slugs and snails will take up residence in the dark, moist spaces under your pots, popping out at night to feast on your vegetables. They love anything juicy and tender, such as lettuce, but young plants of all varieties are vulnerable. I use organically approved slug pellets to keep them at bay, sprinkling them sparingly on the soil and also on the ground around the pots. An active bird population will also help to keep the numbers down, although this of course creates problems in its own right. If at all possible, I recommend getting a toad on your side. I have at least one, possibly two, in residence and they really are a help in getting rid of slimy pests.

WHITEFLY

These small, sap-sucking white insects seem to be most active when plants are grown inside or under cover. The solution is to leave them outside as much as possible. I am a great believer in the health-giving powers of fresh air, and will even put my tender plants outside on mild winter days. Just as with greenfly, a pot of French marigolds or nasturtiums nearby can be an effective preventative measure. If the whitefly do take hold, though, I will resort to spraying with soapy water (see Aphids).

GARDEN & RECIPE NOTES

GARDEN NOTES

The growing guide and gardening advice in this book is based on the experience and climate at Great Dixter house and garden in East Sussex, UK, where summers and winters are generally mild.

The growing guides feature the fruit and vegetables that are grown in various pots in the kitchen courtyard at Great Dixter; do vary these to suit the size of your growing area, the pots you are using and what you like to eat and will use. In terms of choosing what to grow and the failures and successes that follow, it is important to experiment and be willing to try.

Key dates and sowing times are included as a guide. You might need to adapt or vary these depending on the climate where you live. You are also advised to the follow the manufacturer's sowing guidelines on the seed packets.

RECIPE NOTES

Butter is salted, unless specified otherwise.

Eggs are assumed to be large (US extra large) and preferably organic and free-range.

Milk is whole (full-fat) milk, unless specified otherwise.

Pepper is always freshly ground black pepper, unless specified otherwise.

Salt should be a good-quality sea salt, unless specified otherwise.

Herbs are fresh, unless specified otherwise.

Cloves garlic are assumed to be medium; use two if yours are small.

When using the zest of **citrus fruit**, buy unwaxed or organic.

Individual **fruits** and **vegetables**, such as onions and pears, are assumed to be medium size, unless specified otherwise, and should be peeled and/or washed.

Metric, imperial and cup measurements are used in this book. Follow one set of measurements throughout, not a mixture, as they are not interchangeable.

All **spoon and cup measurements** are level, unless otherwise stated. 1 teaspoon = 5 ml; 1 tablespoon = 15 ml. Australian standard tablespoons are 20 ml, so Australian readers are advised to use 3 teaspoons in place of 1 tablespoon when measuring small quantities.

When no quantity is specified, for example, of oils, salts and herbs used for finishing dishes or for deep-frying, quantities are discretionary and flexible.

Cooking and preparation times are for guidance only, as individual ovens vary. If using a convection (fan) oven, follow the manufacturer's directions concerning oven temperatures.

Exercise a high level of caution when following recipes involving any potentially hazardous activity including the use of high temperatures, open flames and when deep-frying. In particular, when deep-frying, add food carefully to avoid splashing, wear long sleeves and never leave the pan unattended.

Some recipes include **raw or very lightly cooked eggs, meat or fish, and fermented products**. These should be avoided by the elderly, infants, pregnant women, convalescents and anyone with an impaired immune system.

When **sterilizing jars or bottles** for preserves, wash them in clean, hot water and rinse thoroughly. Preheat the oven to 140°C/275°F/Gas Mark 1. Place the jars or bottles on a baking sheet and transfer to the oven to dry. Fill the jars or bottles while they are still hot and seal immediately.

When making jams or jellies you will need to **test for setting point**. If using a sugar (candy) thermometer, jams or jellies should register 105°C/220°F. Alternatively, place a saucer in the refrigerator when you start preparing the preserve. At the point specified, place a teaspoonful of the hot juice on the chilled saucer. When cool, it should wrinkle when you push it with your finger. If not, boil a little longer, then test again.

INDEX

Phaidon Press Limited
Regent's Wharf
All Saints Street
London N1 9PA

Phaidon Press Inc.
65 Bleecker Street
New York, NY 10012

phaidon.com

First published 2020
Text © 2020 Aaron Bertelsen and
the Great Dixter Charitable Trust

ISBN 978 0 7148 7861 4

A CIP catalogue record for this book
is available from the British Library
and the Library of Congress.

Commissioning Editor: Victoria Clarke
Project Editors: Clare Churly and
Lucy Kingett
Production Controller: Jane Harman
Designed by Melanie Mues,
Mues Design, London
Photography by Andrew Montgomery

Printed in China

A percentage of the royalties from
the sale of this book will go to
support the Great Dixter Charitable
Trust, which is dedicated to
maintaining the quality and unique
atmosphere of Great Dixter,
protecting the house and its contents
and ensuring that the garden
remains open to inspire visitors with
its exuberant and dynamic style of
gardening. The surrounding estate
with its meadows and ancient
woodland continues to be managed
in the traditional manner to maximize
biodiversity and sustainability.

AUTHOR'S ACKNOWLEDGEMENTS

This book is dedicated to Charles
and Susan Butt. Thank you for your
life-long support.

Thank you to the staff and trustees
of Great Dixter, and to Fergus Garrett.
You are all a part of this book!

My biggest thanks to Louise Bell for
all her help in getting the copy into
order and her ongoing support.

Thank you to Andrew Montgomery
for the photos that make our books
so special.

Thank you to Victoria Clarke, my
editor at Phaidon – I was surprised
that you wanted to do another
book with me! Thank you also to
Lucy Kingett, Clare Churly and Jane
Harman at Phaidon.

Thank you to Bill Thomas and the
board at Chanticleer Garden for
your support.

Thank you to all those who let us take
photos of their container gardens or
generously shared their recipes for
the book.

A big thank you to Mrs Next Door
for everything.

Thank you to my sister Lisa Hayes
for always being there.

Thank you to my wonderful friends
for their support. Some of you went
through a lot: Stuart Alter; Marla
Angermeier; Dan Benarcik; Flora
Bird; Chris Boreham; Lewis Bosher;
Jonny Bruce; Linda Cobb; Ellie and
Stephen Cochrane; Tom and Alex
Coward; Rachel Deacon; Geoffrey and
Susan Dyer; Peter and Olivia Eller;
Edward Flint; Gaye Fox; Peter, Laura
and Kate Gatacre; Jayne Gillespie;
Thomas Gooch; Bill, Nancy and Lee
Hallman; Charlie Harpur; Daimian,
Lisa, Lily, Rico and Kosta Hayes; the
Hnatkiwskyjs; Tobias Holst; Rachael

Howard; Miranda Janatka; Adele and
Simon Johnson; Jill Kowal; Ayala
Landow; Kyle Landt; Andrew Luke;
Jack McCoy; John and Mary Kay
Maksem; David Mattern; Elizabeth
Metcalfe; Belen Moreu; Michael
Morphy; Clara Munoz-Rojas; Matt;
Sammy Pagett; Doreen Payne; Ben
Pick; Lior Pinsky; Mat Reese; May
Reid; Juliet Roberts; Alice, Joe and
Perry Rodriguez; Flora and Johnny
Rothera; Frank and Linda Smith;
Kathy Spagnola; Nigel Spalding;
Cornelia Steffen; James Stewart;
Bill Thomas; Coralie Thomas; Phil
van Huynh; Anthony Wilson; Henry
Witheridge; Jonathan Wright; and
Stephen Zelno.

The publisher would like to thank
the following for their contributions
to the book: Theresa Bebbington,
Louise Bell, Vanessa Bird, Trish
Burgess, Clare Churly, Fergus Garrett,
Eric Guibert and Robin Pembrooke,
Elizabeth Hosking, Kei Ishimaru,
Elaine and Lucy Kingett, Debbie
Major, Fiona and Lionel Meyringer,
Andrew Montgomery, Melanie Mues,
Joanne Murray, Sarah Nuttall and
Louis Wustemann, Joanna Rodgers,
Eddie Royle, Clare Sayer, Christian
Smith, Nigel Spalding and Anthony
Wilson, Bill Thomas, Phil van Huynh
and Julie Weiss.